JN219899

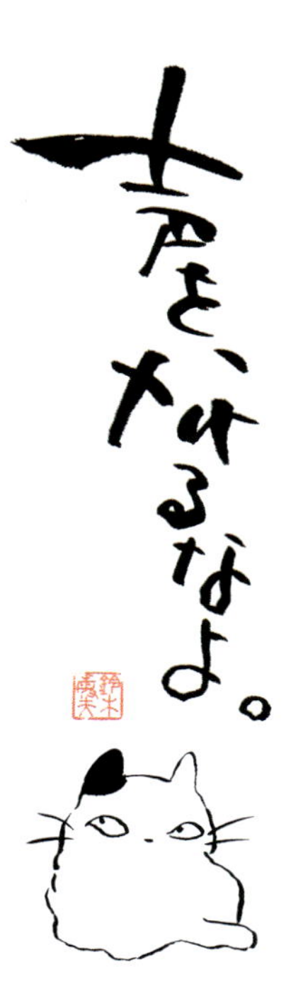


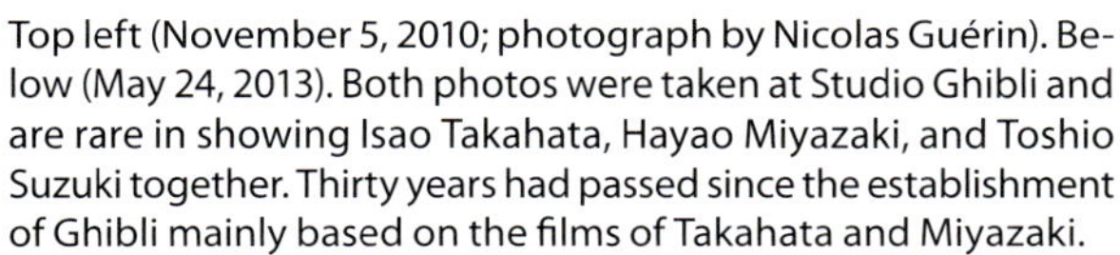
Top left (November 5, 2010; photograph by Nicolas Guérin). Below (May 24, 2013). Both photos were taken at Studio Ghibli and are rare in showing Isao Takahata, Hayao Miyazaki, and Toshio Suzuki together. Thirty years had passed since the establishment of Ghibli mainly based on the films of Takahata and Miyazaki.

This is a drawing by Toshio Suzuki. It was the first drawing by Suzuki to win Miyazaki's praise. The calligraphy reads, *Koe o kakeru na yo* (Don't bother me!)

Toshio Suzuki is well-known for his calligraphy, and it has been employed in various ways in Ghibli films. At top center is the advertising copy for *Kaze tachinu* (The Wind Rises)—*Ikineba* (You must live). At top left is this same calligraphy as seen on a poster for the film. At top right is calligraphy that emulates the work of the Zen Buddhist monk and poet Ryokan (1758–1831), which reads *tenjo taifu* (Big wind in the heavens above), which makes an appearance in *The Wind Rises*.

ゆく河の流れは
絶えずして
しかも、もとの水に
あらず
淀みに浮かぶ
うたかたは
かつ消えかつ結びて
久しくとどまりたる
例なし
世の中にある人と栖と
またかくのごとし

This calligraphy reproduces the opening lines of the 13th-century *Hojoki* (An Account of My Hut). As part of the events celebrating the 800th anniversary of the writing of the *Hojoki*, this calligraphy was displayed in the Shinbukuden of the Shimogamo shrine. It can now be seen at Obuse in Nagano prefecture. The calligraphy reads: "Ceaseless is the change of the water where the stream moves calmly on. Spray flows over the cataracts and is gone without a moment's delay. Such is the fate of man in this world and the houses which he inhabits."

# Mixing Work with Pleasure

## My Life at Studio Ghibli

JAPAN LIBRARY

A sketch by Hayao Miyazaki of Suzuki and Miyazaki sitting side by side. This drawing is one of Suzuki's favorites.

# Mixing Work with Pleasure

## My Life at Studio Ghibli

**Toshio Suzuki**

Translated by
Roger Speares

Japan Publishing Industry Foundation for Culture

**Translation Note**
The Hepburn system of romanization is used for Japanese terms, including the names of persons and places.

*Mixing Work with Pleasure: My Life at Studio Ghibli*
Toshio Suzuki. Translated by Roger Speares

Published by Japan Publishing Industry Foundation for Culture (JPIC)
3-12-3 Kanda-Jinbocho, Chiyoda-ku, Tokyo 101-0051, Japan.

First English edition: March 2018



Originally published in Japanese under the title *Shigoto Doraku Shinpan: Sutajio Jiburi no Genba* by Iwanami Shoten, Publishers, in 2014.

English publishing rights arranged with Iwanami Shoten, Publishers, Tokyo.

Book design by Point & Line Co., Ltd.



Printed in Japan
ISBN 978-4-86658-022-7
http://www.jpic.or.jp/japanlibrary/

Contents

# Preface to the English Edition

What a laugh!
Thirty years of nothing
But high jinks.
(Death poem by one Rikio Ishikawa)

When Hayao Miyazaki announced his retirement, this poem suddenly popped into my head. Some thirty years had also passed since the foundation of the company. About this time I thought of shutting down Ghibli. Looking back, the company had been created to produce the animations of Miyazaki. But a lot of things had become clear in the meantime. Things were not as simple as they seemed. It wasn't easy to give up on something once it had gotten started.

First of all was the question of Ghibli employees. This was a huge concern. If I suddenly called out, "That's it! Ghibli is finished," it would be too self-serving and the height of irresponsibility toward the people working there.

But then I had a thought. Yes, given the circumstances, I should find a successor. I could force the responsibility on him. The problem would be solved. Just as thoughts like this were going through my mind, Miyazaki suddenly announced, out of the blue, that he was not retiring after all.

He had done everything he could possibly do. He had given it his heart and soul, and that's why he was quitting. That was the reason he gave when he announced his retirement. And it made sense. I had been working closely with Miya-san for forty years. I had seen how seriously he devoted himself to his work, day after grueling day. Consequently, what he said was convincing. And Ghibli had shut down its production department. Then, barely two years later, just two years, he changed his mind.

"Hey, give me a break!" I thought, but it was already too late. He brought over storyboards worth twenty minutes of screen time and asked me to take a look at them. The expression on his face was more serious than I had ever seen before.

"If you don't think it's interesting, just tell me frankly," he said. "I'll give it up."

He was saying he would leave the decision entirely in my hands. His manner of speaking was polite and even modest, but on closer consideration I think it was a form of intimidation or even a threat. From the start he knew I wouldn't say anything against it.

Sakes alive! What am I supposed to do?

Where had my dreams of a happy life in retirement gone?

A famous director grows old and produces flops. Many directors have trodden this path. I didn't want to see that happen here. That's why I had viewed his retirement in a positive light. So it was with a trembling heart that I ran my eyes over the storyboards. Anxiety and hope crisscrossed my mind. But before I realized it, I had been drawn into the world unfolding before me.

"Shall we do it?"

As I spoke, Miya-san's face took on a reddish tinge.

The title was *Kimitachi wa do ikiruka* (How Do You Live?) The content, however, was quite different from the title. It was fantasy on a grand scale. Reading the story, I could understand very well why Miya-san had re-emerged from retirement. He didn't want to end with *The Wind Rises*. All said and done, his real love was adventure fantasy.

That decided, I couldn't spend my time making preparations to shut down Ghibli. Instead, I undertook a major restructuring of the company.

At present Ghibli is working on two simultaneous feature films, the one by Miya-san and the other under the direction of his son, Goro. Miya-san is using traditional hand-drawn techniques, while Goro is using computer graphics. Aside from that, discussing matters with Miya-san, we are planning the next film.

Ghibli would continue to make films. That is its mission. That is what it does—until the very last day of its existence. I steeled myself for whatever the future might bring. Further, I took a hand in personnel decisions.

Time and tide wait for no man. Koji Hoshino had been president of Ghibli for ten years. Kiyofumi Nakajima had been serving as director of the Ghibli Museum for twelve and a half. As a matter of course, the organization had lost its flexibility. So I had Hoshino become chairman and Nakajima the new president. To fill Nakajima's shoes Kazuki Anzai was appointed the head of Ghibli Museum, the first time for a woman to serve in that post and the highlight of the personnel changes.

On top of all that, it was decided to build a Ghibli theme park in my hometown of Nagoya.

The rebirth of Studio Ghibli! A fresh breeze blew through the company. The personnel reshuffling produced an in-house vitality beyond anything we had imagined. The staff was re-energized.

In conclusion, I would like to note the names and ages of the principal figures at Ghibli.

Isao Takahata, 82
Hayao Miyazaki, 76
Toshio Suzuki, 69
Koji Hoshino, 61

Kiyofumi Nakajima, 54
Kazuki Anzai, 52
Goro Miyazaki, 50

Toshio Suzuki
Producer and Chairman
Studio Ghibli
November 28, 2017

# Preface to the Revised Japanese Edition

Among Ingmar Bergman's films is one called *Tystnaden* (The Silence). It caused quite a stir in Japan when it was first released: was it art or was it smut? I was a freshman in high school at the time, and since the movie was banned for those under the age of eighteen, I could only dream of seeing it. Then one of my friends said, "But we can see the trailer!"

That's how we came to see *Tom Jones*. Our motives for seeing the movie were not of the purest kind. We didn't particularly want to see *Tom Jones*, but only the preview that preceded it. It turned out, however, that *Tom Jones* would be a turning point in my life, proving that life is deeper than we think. The movie is a comedy-adventure portraying the love life and escapades of a young man. I became infatuated with the protagonist and fell under the influence of his honest, kindhearted way of life.

Around the same time, a song by Hitoshi Ueki, *Damatte ore ni tsuite koi* (Shaddup and Stick with Me) became wildly popular. Here are a few of the lyrics:

*Got no money? Come and see me.*
*I ain't got any either, but not to worry.*
*Just look! The blue sky, the white clouds.*
*Somehow things'll turn out fine.*

This was right in the middle of the rapid economic growth period, and Japanese were working as hard as bees and starting to go a little funny in the head. This is precisely when Ueki's song appeared on the scene, with its unfounded optimism that things would turn out all right in the end. It was a lifesaver. "Somehow things'll turn out fine" was on everyone's lips.

A movie can change a man's life; a song can change people's worldview. I wanted to do work like that. Just for a moment I caught a glimpse of the future. Checking up on it, I see that both of these events took place in 1964, fifty years ago.

Toshio Suzuki
May 2014

# About the Japanese Revised Edition

The original Japanese version of this book, *Shigoto doraku: Sutajio Jiburi no genba* (lit. Mixing Work with Pleasure: On Site at Studio Ghibli), was published on July 18, 2008. On May 5, 2014, a revised edition was published, and a new chapter (chapter 8) was added, which mainly concerns Hayao Miyazaki's activities following the release of his *Gake no ue no Ponyo* (Ponyo on the Cliff by the Sea; July 2008). Emendations in chapters 1 to 7 of the original edition were kept to a minimum in the revised edition, and chronological references have been basically left as they were. This English translation is based on the 2014 revised edition.

The publication of the revised edition was spurred by several factors: Hayao Miyazaki's announcement of his retirement from feature animation film in September 2013 following the release of *Kaze tachinu* (The Wind Rises; July 2013); Isao Takahata's return to animation after a fourteen-year hiatus with the release of *Kaguya-hime no monogatari* (The Tale of The Princess Kaguya; November 2013); Toshio Suzuki's appointment to the position of general manager at Studio Ghibli in March 2014; and finally, the thirtieth anniversary of *Kaze no tani no Naushika* (Nausicaä of the Valley of the Wind), which had proved the impetus for the establishing of Studio Ghibli.

(Editorial Department, Iwanami Shinsho)

# In Place of a Preface: Memories Never to be Forgotten

It never occurred to me to look back on my working life and try to organize things and put them into some kind of order. Somehow I couldn't help feeling that to do so would take me away from real work, away from the workplace.

So I never made an effort to remember what I had done previously. In fact, I thought it best to forget the past, and sometimes I even made a deliberate effort to do just that. My personal motto was, "Starting afresh produces the best results."

What caused me to think in this way I am not really sure, but it may have been my reading of the poetry of Kenji Miyazawa during my college days, or it may have been the influence of the poet and playwright Shuji Terayama. In my own way I learned from them that what is done is done; it is the present, living moment that is of utmost importance.

It is this moment, what is immediately before your eyes, that is crucial. The past is of no concern. For the last thirty years I have been talking with Hayao Miyazaki (nicknamed "Miya-san") almost every day, but we have never once talked about the past. It is always the present. We talk about what has to be done right now, or what has to be done a year from now. Even so, we always have a ton of things to talk about.

Miya-san is a past master at forgetting things, and I think this is not unconnected to the secret of his filmmaking. With someone of his accomplishments, ordinarily you would expect him to build on his past achievements as he moves from film to film. You would expect him to polish and refine his techniques and devices to a greater level of perfection.

But this is not what happens with Miya-san. He attacks each new film as if he were a novice director. This might be due to his uniqueness as a creator, but it might also be due to his forgetfulness.

I recall the novelist Junnosuke Yoshiyuki saying something like, "Memories that you forget are not important memories." That is, there are two types of memories: those that permeate your being and those that fade and disappear. Memories that slip your mind unless you have committed them to writing in a notebook or a diary are not worth remembering. Now I only have a vague recollection of Yoshiyuki's exact words, but the important thing, I think, is that their meaning has become a part of my inner being.

In my position as a producer, there are many important factors in my work, such as what kind of advertising copy I have made in the past, what were the conditions for the commercial tie-ins I negotiated, what were the relevant precedents. But these are things that it is all right to forget. If necessary, you can always ask someone, or you can check past records. That is usually enough to refresh your memory.

When there is a tool available for remembering things, you should make use of that tool. That is why we have records. But records and memory are different things. Human memory has its limits, I believe, so what is available should, as much as possible, be used only for important things. That's why I try to keep memories of what I have done in the past to a minimum.

As part of my job I spend a lot of time talking with people in interviews and on talk shows. In the midst of these conversations I sometimes change the topic or broaden it by saying, "Oh, that reminds me of something." This is the truth. I have often had this experience, suddenly recalling something in the middle of a conversation, or recollecting something long forgotten when asked a question. This happens because the particular "memory" has permeated my being. It is usually not something that I have made an effort to commit to memory but something that has somehow become a part of me.

So what I write here may not be strictly accurate in terms of who did what and when; the order of events may be slightly off. What is important, I think, is the content of what is remembered. For instance, in mathematics we are taught that 55 plus 44 is 99, that 2,050 plus 1,030 is 3,080. But isn't it more important to remember that, overall, the sums add up to about 100 and approximately 3,000?

It has been thirty years since I became involved in the world of animation with the launching of the monthly magazine *Animeju* (Animage), and more than twenty years since the establishment of Studio Ghibli (as of 2008). The important memories of that time have become thoroughly my own, and here I will try to depict what those memories are. I will present them as I recall them, just as they were.

You will have to forgive me if the narrative sometimes seems to go astray, jumping from topic to topic, for my mind seems deluged by so many things. I have no idea if what I write will be interesting or useful to the reader, and can only ask that each person takes from the book what suits his or her needs.

# 1 Mixing Work with Pleasure/ Trust Means Total Trust

## The *Animage* Era

The author, Toshio Suzuki, as a long-haired college student.

**Toshio Suzuki**

---

It was around the end of March 1978 when Hideo Ogata asked me out for a cup of tea. He was notoriously cheap, and so when he said, "I'll pay," I took it as a danger signal. And I was right. This little incident proved to be a life-changer.

"You know that the first issue of *Animage* is scheduled to be published on May 26, right? I'd like you to handle it..."

"Huh? What?" I was at a loss for words. After all, I knew that Ogata had been laying careful plans for the first Japanese animation information magazine with an outside production company for more than six months.

It was about that production company. "I canned all those guys sometime last year," he said.

For the second time I found myself at a loss for words. Still, I tried to keep calm. I replied, "That's easy to say, but there are less than two months left to the pub date."

Ogata was famous for springing ideas on people, I knew, but that didn't prevent me from being totally dumbstruck.

("Koshi kondo no hito" [A Man Who Mixes Work with Pleasure], in *Ano hata o ute!* [Fire on that Flag!], Hideo Ogata; 2004)

---

### Getting Started at *Asahi Geino*

I joined the publisher Tokuma Shoten in 1972. I was first assigned to the weekly magazine *Asahi Geino*. Until then I hadn't been in the habit of reading weekly magazines, but once I got started I found that it was an interesting world. Its ironclad rules were pounded into me—conducting interviews conscientiously, viewing things from different angles, and acting quickly—all of which I still find valid today.

*Asahi Geino* had two departments: planning or regular features and one-off special features. I was assigned to the planning/regular features department and put in charge of the page that dealt with topics like fortunetelling and manga. The head of planning/regular features was the previously mentioned Hideo Ogata, a man who possessed fascinating charm. Unfortunately, he passed away in 2007.

The next year I became the editor of *Komikku & Komikku* (Comic & Comic), the supplement to *Asahi Geino*. It was there that I got on friendly terms with manga artists like Osamu Tezuka, Shotaro Ishinomori, and George Akiyama. Thereafter I moved to the special features department of *Asahi Geino*, and nearly every week I was kept as busy as a worker bee writing the four-page special feature. Among the articles I wrote, a piece that still stands out in my mind is the one titled "Motorcycle Gangs and Kamikaze Pilots." The issue coincided with the day commemorating the end of the war; it was meant to connect "then" with "now," combining coverage of the wartime "special attack unit" (*tokkotai*) with the motorcycle gangs who were much in the news at the time. Among the men who served in the naval air force, there were many who played an active part in the kamikaze corps, and there were others who weren't called into action before this critical period ended. When I asked the former kamikaze what they thought about the motorcycle gangs, their opinions were clearly divided. Those who had survived the missions said they could understand the motorcycle gangs. Those who had not actually taken part in a mission were largely negative. In any case, I couldn't help but be impressed by these men who had once given up on life. At first, they weren't forthcoming. In some cases, it was only after we had been talking for eight hours or so that they began to open up.

Covering the motorcycle gangs was really interesting. They gathered at a coffee shop they had reserved, and just as I was wondering what they were going to do, the coffee shop was transformed into a kind of free-discussion classroom like a "homeroom," where students exchange opinions and thoughts about school life. For example, some said that girls shouldn't ride on the back of the bikes, which some girls objected to. "We have a reporter with us today," someone said, and their talk became very serious. They brought up particular cases concerning how to deal with the police, saying, "If you go too far, you can be accused of interfering with an officer in the pursuit of his duties, so be careful." I was privileged to witness exchanges like this.

Before analyzing an event, it is best to go to the actual scene. You can discover something new there. I learned this from my weekly magazine work, a very important experience.

### I Had Only Three Weeks!

Back to the spring of 1978, the time when *Animage* was launched.

First I would like to make some corrections to the text of "The Man Who Mixes Work with Pleasure," mentioned above. I was invited to tea not in March, but in April—and just before the spring holidays at that. The dustup with the production company had taken place not the year before, but the day before. The magazine was to be launched not in two months' time, but in three weeks!

Why the discrepancies? The text quoted above appeared in Ogata's 2004 book *Ano hata o ute! Animeju keppu-roku* (Fire on that Flag! The Bloody Chronicles of *Animage*), which included short essays from those in the industry, such as Isao Takahata and Hayao Miyazaki. To be brief and to the point, these discrepancies were a result of Ogata's self-serving rewriting. He didn't want the real slipshod nature of the project to be known, so he manipulated the dates. After asking me to write something for the book, he went ahead and changed the most important part. This type of thing didn't bother him at all. He was that kind of person. I will take advantage of this opportunity to set the record straight.

At the time I was in charge of a children's television magazine called *Gekkan terebi rando* (Monthly TV Land), and *Animage* was intended to be a supplement to that magazine. So it was not unreasonable for Ogata to ask me to take on *Animage*. But even though it was just supposed to be a supplement, the title did contain the word "monthly," so it was equivalent to the launch of a new magazine. From the third volume, the word "supplement" was removed, making it in name and fact an independent publication. Even getting it ready in two months would have been beyond reason, and three weeks was absolutely absurd. That was the situation.

One thing that really impressed me was the title *Animage*. It was a contraction of the English "animation" and the French "image." Coming up with a title like this was very typical of Ogata. He was a genius in this respect. Later on, Isao Takahata said he was also much taken with the title.

## The Rest Is Up to You

What happened after that? Here I will quote again from "A Man Who Mixes Work with Pleasure," mentioned above.

> *After that, there was an exchange of "I want you to do it," and "No, it's impossible." There just wasn't enough time or manpower, I thought. As we were talking, however, I suddenly realized I had fallen into a trap. Somehow it was decided that I would take on the*

*project. "About the staff, I'll get what you want," he said, "but I'll be editor-in-chief myself."*

*Up until then I had been working on a TV magazine for children, which was not unconnected to animation. Still, I wasn't brimming with confidence. After all, in less than two months I had to create Japan's first full-fledged animation magazine.*

*"What's the editorial policy?" I asked.*

*"Well, you know," he said, "my son likes animation, so I'd like it to be a high-quality book for smart kids."*

*I now regretted that I had accepted the job, but it was already too late. Ogata was a very naive person, if nothing else.*

*"What is there beyond that?" I asked.*

*"The feature article should be on* Uchu senkan Yamato *(Space Battleship Yamato). My son's a big fan, so this is a must. The rest is up to you."*

As I said, the two months mentioned here was actually three weeks.

I can laugh about it now, but at the time I was frantic. Since the magazine was supposed to go on sale in three weeks, the actual time we had for work was only about two weeks. If you included the time for preparing the manuscripts and getting them ready for the printer, that left only about a week for research and interviews. This is what it means to be unimaginably busy, I supposed.

The first day was devoted to background study and recruiting people. I had to have a staff as soon as humanly possible. I located only five prospects among company employees, and I increased that to ten or so by asking around among freelancers I had connections with. At the same time I had to do some quick background research. True, I had been in charge of *Monthly TV Land*, but that dealt mostly with manga, not animation. About animation I knew practically nothing. Ogata introduced me to a high school girl who knew a lot about the subject, and I started studying under her tutelage, but this lasted only one day. On the second day I had to start making a flat plan of the magazine, including a table of contents. On the third day there was an editorial meeting.

I am not the type who remembers the details of past work, who did what and when. But in this case I remember everything, on a day-by-day basis.

## Mixing Work with Pleasure: The Rest Is Up to You

The all-important editorial policy was simple: "I'd like it to be a high-quality book for smart kids; my son's a big fan of *Space Battleship Yamato*."

"Oh," I thought. "He's doing it for his own son. It's alright to mix work with pleasure." Somehow, amid all the busyness, that took a load off my shoulders.

In the end, Ogata's words provided a useful hint. The fact that the price of the magazine was set at 580 yen came from his notion that the magazine should be of high quality. At the time the going price for a magazine never went over 500 yen, so 580 yen was exorbitant. Another main feature of editorial policy was its emphasis on interviews with the people who did the drawing and direction. This also had its roots in Ogata's notion that the magazine should be for "smart kids." The interviews shouldn't be superficial or insipid, but would tell the real story.

Looking back, nothing seems simpler than being told that everything is up to you—"You can do what you want, you can decide the price and book size, you can determine the content"—but it wasn't all that easy. Even in the best of times, you can't help worrying about the progress of ongoing work. You would pop in and ask things like "How's it going?"

But Ogata really did place everything in your hands. While the rest of us invariably worked late into the night, he'd leave for home in the evening, saying, "I'm counting on you."

Ogata didn't look at anything until the press proof. In fact, he didn't even look at that very closely, just the final printed sample. There aren't many chief editors who are that hands-off.

As it happened, the first issue of *Animage* had a printing of 70,000 copies, all of which sold out in three days.

## The Greatness of the Man Who Lights the Fire

From the above you may think that Ogata was nothing but a smooth talker, and did nothing himself. But that wasn't the case at all. Here I quote again from "A Man Who Mixes Work with Pleasure."

> *"Ideas, ideas, ideas" was the mantra that was always on his lips. He was invariably interested in what was new, a very inquisitive person. Though he was often misunderstood, many of his ideas were absolutely stupendous. Perhaps his greatest contribution was to suggest that "we make* Nausicaä *into a film." Being the type of person he was, he didn't consider the consequences of what he was saying. Even when everyone thought an idea was ridiculous, he would mark it down to a lack of imagination and keep saying, "Let's do it. Let's do it." Then, when we had finally gotten to work on the project, his mind had already turned to something else. Grabbing hold of other staff members, he would start discussing a new idea.*
>
> *That's the kind of person he was.*
>
> *I didn't realize it then, but I do now—in fact, I was working side by side with a genius, an exemplary producer. He was like someone who kindles a fire where nothing existed before, an instigator and an initiator. A producer needs that kind of character.*
>
> *The fact that Ogata wasn't good at the day-to-day details gave the rest of us the opportunity to learn a great deal. Foremost was the notion that it was acceptable to mix work with pleasure. It all comes down to this. After that was the fact that once he asked you to do something, he left everything in your hands.*

Left: The cover of the first issue of *Animage*, which was produced in the unimaginably short time of three weeks. Extravagantly colored, it even featured three shades of black.

マンガ映画の魔術師
宮崎 駿 みやざきはやお
冒険とロマンの世界

宮崎氏が構想中の新作のイメージボードより

宮さんがマンガ映画で果たしたいと思っている夢ってあるでしょう。いまの宮さんには、冒険があり夢があり、少年たちを勇気づける善意のマンガ映画を実現しうる、すべてのノウハウとエネルギーがあるんですね。　（大塚康生）

25

Right: The early special feature in *Animage* devoted to Hayao Miyazaki (August 1981). The illustration shows the concept sketch that would later come to fruition in *Nausicaä of the Valley of the Wind*. At that time the scene was set in the civil war period characterized by clashes between samurai clans.

About *Nausicaä* I will have more to say later. Here I would like to relate some episodes that occurred during this *Asahi Geino* period.

If Ogata liked someone, he would immediately ask them to write something, no matter who they might be. At that time, the ratio of special pages to regular pages was supposed to be seven to three, but that was turned on its head while Ogata was in charge. He wouldn't give a thought to what the character of the magazine was supposed to be; everything that had been accepted as a given until then was thrown to the wind. But from this something remarkable would emerge. Take Kazumasa Hirai. Ogata kept pestering him to write something, and I think it's fair to say that's what turned Hirai into a novelist. At one point there was a long series by the poet and playwright Shuji Terayama, and this too was Ogata's doing. Ogata was on very friendly terms with some surprising people, such as the actors Bunta Sugawara and Rentaro Mikuni.

## In Any Case, an Interesting Character

I'd like to say a little more about Hideo Ogata, a person about whom interesting stories abound. During the *Asahi Geino* era a man named Osamu Kameyama was working with me and was a very valuable asset. This was about the time we were trying to make *Nausicaä* into an animated film. I suppose the statute of limitations has run out on this story, so I think it's alright to tell it. Kameyama didn't have an official position or title then, and I asked Ogata to see that he got one. Ogata said, "I was thinking the same thing." From that point on, the story took a typical Ogata turn.

"What should his title be, I wonder," he said.

"Maybe *shunin*," I suggested.

"No, *desuku* for sure," he replied.

The company hierarchy ran from *shunin* to *kakari-cho* and then *kacho*, followed by *jicho* and *bucho*. *Desuku* was the same as *jicho*. From an organizational point of view, jumping from the position of a titleless nonentity to *jicho* was unthinkable. But that's what Ogata said he would propose at the board of directors meeting.

The meeting over, Ogata came back, looking thoroughly disappointed. He told me, "It didn't work out."

"What didn't work out?"

"*Jicho*, they won't make him a *jicho*," he said.

What did you expect? I think to myself.

"They say the best they can do is *shunin*," he continued.

That's what I suggested in the first place, so what's wrong with *shunin*, I thought—it's a happy ending. But since Ogata had proposed the position of *jicho*, that was all he was thinking about. In his own mind he had failed. He even went so far as to apologize to Kameyama, who, much like anyone else in the same situation, was unsure how to respond.

Another peculiarity of Ogata's was the seating of his staff in the office. It depended on his personal likes and dislikes. Those he liked sat nearer to his desk; those he didn't like sat further away. Though the office space was the property of the magazine, he managed to pull off these kinds of infantile antics.

This type of thing cropped up time and again. It sometimes led to confusion, but it was, no denying it, very interesting.

I doubt that I will ever meet another person like Ogata. At the end of "A Man Who Mixes Work with Pleasure" I wrote: "Unfortunately, I still haven't reached his level yet," and I meant what I said. As a matter of fact, I can't help feeling that whatever scale I have attained as a human being is due to having worked under him.

As it turned out, my working on the launch of *Animage* proved not only an invaluable experience but an important turning point in my life. Thanks to the established editorial policy of conducting interviews with animators and directors, I met Isao Takahata and Hayao Miyazaki.

# 2 The Importance of Shared Interests in Relationships

## Meeting Isao Takahata and Hayao Miyazaki

The cover of a collection of concept sketches from *Taiyo no oji Horusu no daiboken* (The Little Norse Prince Valiant; Tokuma Shoten, 2003). The concept sketch is by Hayao Miyazaki.

**Toshio Suzuki**

---

I started out at a publishing company, so I can be called an editorial-type producer. What is an editorial-type producer? It is someone who gets the author of a work to bring the project to completion. That is an editorial-type producer's main job. To do this it is important that the editor and the author share something in common, that they be compatible. But more than this, it is the producer's job to act as the first reader of what the author is trying to create. This standpoint is of utmost importance.

What does it mean to be the author's first reader? The most important point is the editor's initial response when an author approaches him with something new. If the editor mistakes the timing here, communications will break down. To respond in the right way, the editor has to know the author's cultural and intellectual background. If he doesn't, he has to acquire it.

(*Eiga doraku* [Mixing Film with Pleasure]; 2005)

---

## Turned Down after an Hour and a Half

I came to know Isao Takahata and Hayao Miyazaki during the throes of launching *Animage*. I have already written elsewhere about our relationship from our first meeting to the completion of *Nausicaä*, so there would seem little need to go over it again, but since it is a seminal point in my life I will say a little more here.

As the person responsible for everyday operations in launching *Animage*, I somehow had to produce a full-fledged magazine despite the lack of time. Thinking how I could possibly fill 118 pages, it occurred to me that I could get at least eight pages by taking up past classics. My motives were not entirely pure in this regard, needless to say.

The high school girl who was acting as my tutor told me that *The Little Norse Prince Valiant* (1968) was absolutely fantastic. I immediately called Isao Takahata, who had been the director. It was then that I got the shock of my life. At the time, if I remember correctly, Takahata was working with Hayao Miyazaki on the animation *Mirai Shonen Konan* (The Future Boy Conan; 1978), and they both happened to be together in the staff room when I called. The only thing I said to Takahata was that I would like to meet him, but he started on an endless explanation of why that wouldn't be possible. He went on for an hour! I was dumbfounded.

Exactly what he said then I don't really remember. But they thought my magazine was riding on a wave of popularity created by *Space Battleship Yamato*, and he said something to the effect that they couldn't collaborate in the creation of a general magazine, that they had serious doubts about lending their support to such an undertaking. Now, looking back, I wish that I had committed his train of thought to memory.

In any case, I was rather amazed that a person should take an hour just to say that he didn't want to meet me. Just as I was thinking, "Well, it can't be helped. I'll just have to give up on any meeting,"

Takahata concluded his rant by saying, "That's why I can't agree to an interview, but there is Hayao Miyazaki, who worked with me on *The Little Norse Prince Valiant*. He is sitting next to me right now, and he may be of a different opinion. If you want, I'll put him on the line." After rambling on about why he didn't want to take part, now he was offering to introduce me to someone else! Was this kindness or what? I was mystified.

This was the first time for me to hear the name Hayao Miyazaki (later we simply called him Miya-san). He started by saying, "I've got the general idea. Here is what I think." He had apparently been listening to my conversation with Takahata. The only thing I could say was, "Uh-huh."

He went on, "I have a ton of things I want to say about *The Little Norse Prince Valiant*. I want sixteen pages."

What I had originally asked from Takahata was simply a few comments in the middle of an eight-page spread. Now Miyazaki was asking for sixteen pages or he wouldn't do it. What a strange pair of characters!

This would become clear later on, but *The Little Norse Prince Valiant* had special meaning for both of them; it was a product of their days at the production company Toei Animation, where they had been organizers in the labor and union movement. Not only was the film a high point in the history of animated feature film in Japan, it was also a reflection of their younger days. That's why Miya-san felt he needed sixteen pages to say all he had to say about the film's background. As I would learn later on, Miya-san was adept at reducing everything to numbers, but in this case "sixteen pages" was apparently just off the top of his head.

In the end I talked with Takahata for an hour and Miyazaki for about a half hour—an hour and a half altogether! I was completely exhausted and I finally gave up. Actually, there was no time left. I didn't have the leeway to be quibbling with these two. Left with little choice, I said, as politely as I could, "Well, if that's the situation, I will withdraw my request."

Given their unique characters, I was seriously impressed by these two, and I couldn't get *The Little Norse Prince Valiant* off my mind, even though I hadn't seen it yet. Back then, of course, there wasn't anything available in a video format. There were theaters devoted to classic films, but who could say when *The Little Norse Prince Valiant* would be shown? As it happened, sometime after launching *Animage* I heard that the Bungei-za in Ikebukuro was going to be showing the film as part of an all-night event. I rushed off in the middle of the night to see it. It was totally mindblowing.

The backdrop of the film was the Vietnam War. My generation was steeped in politics, and it was easy to see that the story about the defense of a village against a powerful foe was based on that conflict. The film was suffused with the thoughts and emotions of that period. So animation was capable of something like this! I was totally amazed, and I felt more strongly than ever that I wanted to meet its creators.

### Just Sitting Next to Him

I first met Miya-san just as he had started work on *Rupan sansei: Kariosutoro no shiro* (The Castle of Cagliostro, 1979). Osamu Kameyama, my colleague at *Animage*, had gone to see Miyazaki, but had gotten the cold shoulder. He sent me an SOS, and so the next time I went with him. Miya-san simply said, "I don't want to be interviewed," and clamped his mouth shut. Left with no other alternative, Kameyama and I brought over a couple of stools and sat next to him. "Don't sit there," Miyazaki said. "You're in the way." It was going to be a test of wills. Kameyama and I kept sitting there, but Miya-san didn't say a word.

As we sat there watching him, we found that he kept working until about two in the morning. When he finally finished his work, I asked him what time he would start the next day, and he said nine o'clock. He had only four months to finish *The Castle of Cagliostro* drawings, but even so, Miya-san was a terribly hard worker.

We decided to stick it out and follow his schedule, and we hung around until 2:00 a.m. and showed up at nine the next morning. We sat next to him just watching, not saying a word. I don't recall how many days passed like this, maybe a week. Then, for the first time, he showed us the storyboards. It was the car chase scene.

Miyazaki suddenly asked, "What do you call this here?" Kameyama, who was a fan of professional cycling, immediately responded, "I think it's called *makuru*, 'overtaking.'"

"Ah, I see," Miyazaki said, and he wrote the word on the storyboard. The word is still there, as you can see from the storyboards on page 39. This seemed to break the dam, and the words came rushing out of Miyazaki's mouth. That was to be our fateful meeting, so to speak. I have a clear memory of the scene. As for Miyazaki himself, he still says, "What a pair of shady characters, I thought at the time." In the end, though, we just seemed to get along.

## My First Meeting with Isao Takahata

The opportunity to meet Isao Takahata came not long after the encounter with Miya-san. I had heard that he was going to make a new animated feature film based on the manga *Jarinko Chie* (Chie the Brat) by Etsumi Haruki (the film was released in 1981). As soon as I heard the news, I rushed off to see him.

About a ten-minute walk from Koenji station near Yamato Rikkyo, there was a company called Telecom, which was where the production work would be done. I was to be introduced to Takahata by Yasuo Otsuka, a colleague of Takahata's at Toei Animation—a very nice person—who said, "There's a coffee shop out in front; it might be best to talk there." Takahata and I went out as directed, but there was nary a coffee shop in sight! We walked and walked until we finally came across one. Sitting down, the first words out of Takahata's mouth were, "I suppose you want to ask the usual trivial questions, like what did I like about the original manga, what led me to want to do an animation, and so on." He was looking for a fight from the start. That really ticked me off, I can tell you.

Even though this was our first meeting, we talked for over three hours. Before I knew it we were discussing the production and content of the film. I was still young and smart-alecky in those days and didn't hesitate to say, "After producing a classic like *Arupusu no shojo Haiji* [Heidi, A Girl of the Alps; 1974], how can you now do a film about a girl cooking giblets on skid row in Osaka? It's not consistent with your other work."

That made him mad. "It's consistent in my own mind," he shot back. "What makes you say something like that? What gave you that idea?" That's about how the conversation went.

After we had finished talking, Takahata concluded by saying something I still remember. "So there. I doubt you can make sense of what I've said. If you think you can, give it a try."

It was a kind of challenge. "Okay, I'll give it a shot," I said. And when I wrote up the interview, it did make sense.

In any case, thanks to this meeting, I learned what an interesting person Takahata was. I began to drop by his studio every day, even when there was no need to do so.

## Taking Part in Animation Production

From the very beginning Takahata and I talked about the plot of the film. Since I didn't want to be put in the position of not being able to keep up with him, I decided to learn everything I could about the manga *Chie the Brat*. At the time it consisted of about eight volumes, I think. I read them all very carefully and learned all the dialogue by

| カット | 画面 | 内容 | | 秒 |
|---|---|---|---|---|
| 92 | | Follow(BG動画)<br>Fiatの前へ<br>コンコン コンと<br>はずんでいく<br>ワオッとなって<br>よけるルパン<br>(2.0) | キ〜ッ | |
| | | 空中で<br>炸裂 | ドガーン | |
| | | 爆煙 うしろへ<br>流れていく.<br>千鳥足になって<br>蛇行する<br>そこへ, すぐ<br>もう一発 | キ〜ッ | |
| | | 今度は もろに<br>爆煙につつまれる | ドガーン | |
| | | 流れ去るケムリの<br>中から,<br>煙をひきずって<br>出てくる Fiat<br>フロントガラス ヌリ<br>(ヒビわれちゃって) | キ〜ッ | 7.0 |

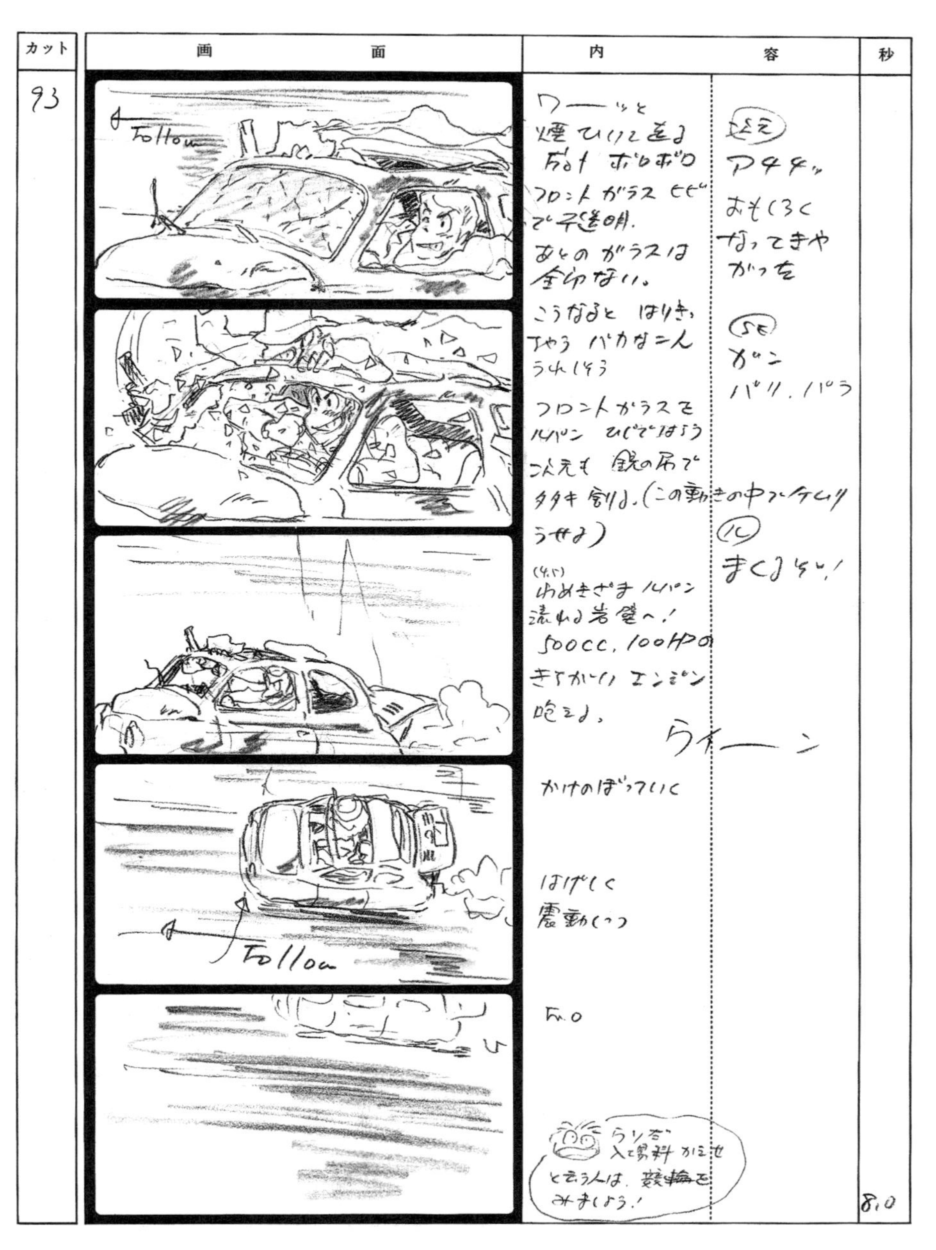


Car chase scene, storyboards from *The Castle of Cagliostro*. The word *makuru,* inserted by Miyazaki, can still be seen in scene #93.

heart. And one more thing: since animation is essentially a series of individual drawings, I studied the positioning of the characters in each frame. If I was going to keep company with Takahata, this much was essential. Otherwise, I couldn't get the better of him in an argument.

At that time the scenario hadn't been finished. As I learned later, Takahata was the type who couldn't bring himself to finalize the screenplay or storyboards. For example, in the original manga there is a scene where Chie and her mother meet. I thought this was the most moving moment in the book, but it was missing from Takahata's scenario. I pointed this out to him, going on pretty vehemently about how this was precisely the scene that readers would like to see most and should therefore be included. But he wouldn't agree. He replied, rather illogically, that if the author, Etsumi Haruki, had been in good health at the time, he would never have included this scene. How absurd, I thought. Later on, though, I made use of this logic myself, and repeated the story to others.

In any case, somewhere along the line our relationship became more than simply that of director and magazine editor, and I began to take part in the production process. Going on like this day after day eventually had an adverse effect on the film's progress. After all, I was taking the director away from his work. The producer reprimanded me any number of times, telling me not to take Takahata away from the studio so often; it was slowing down work on the film.

In time the film was brought to completion, and I was invited to the party celebrating the event. There, to my amazement, Takahata greeted me with a deep bow. He said, "Our talks were of tremendous help. Thanks to you, the direction of the film was established. I want to express my appreciation." That pleased me to no end. In hindsight, maybe that was my first step toward becoming a producer.

## Sharing a Common Perspective

My initial meet-ups with Takahata and Miyazaki were momentous events, and I naturally thought I would like to get to know them better. In order to do that, I would have to familiarize myself with their way of thinking. To be unable to converse on an equal footing would be very frustrating.

First of all, making use of my background as a magazine reporter, I began to take down everything they said in my reporter's notebook. This would be the fastest way of getting to know them well, I thought—in fact, the only way. So I began frantically making notes of whatever they said. The way they spoke, the peculiarities of their speech, were also important, so I tried to capture what they said exactly in the way they said it. It wasn't easy, I can tell you. Miya-san spoke very rapidly, and Takahata was very long-winded, invariably going on for three hours.

After we parted, I would go to a coffee shop and put my notes in order. There were places where something was missing, and other places I didn't understand. Racking my brains, I would fill in the gaps. Returning home, I would transcribe it all into a notebook. So, in all, I went over these notes a total of three times.

I was meeting with Miyazaki and Takahata almost every day, but still I kept up this regime. My sleeping time was drastically curtailed, but I was young then, just in my early thirties, and in any case I felt compelled to carry on if I wanted to be their equal. Even after I began to collaborate with them in making films, I still continued the habit of taking notes on our conversations until nearly the end of the eighties. By then, however, I had discontinued transcribing the notes.

Often they would ask if I had read a certain book. In my capacity as an editor, I was in the habit of reading many types of books, and in any event I was fond of reading. But the books they recommended were not the usual kind. If I hadn't read them, I figured, I would have nothing to say if they came up in conversation. One book that Takahata often mentioned was André Bazin's *Qu'est-ce que le cinéma?* (What is Cinema?), a Japanese translation of which was published by Bijutsu Shuppansha in four boxed volumes. Then there was Donald Richie's *Viewing Film*. Before reading Richie's book, I didn't understand what was interesting about Stanley Kubrick's *Barry Lyndon*. When I read that the poor acting was what was good about the film, that the movie was a kind of fabricated documentary, I felt as though a veil had been lifted from my eyes. It is now one of my favorite films. I read Richie's book over and over until it was in tatters. Later, a reprinted Japanese edition (*Eiga no doko o do yomu ka*) was published by Studio Ghibli.

Among the books I hadn't read was one that Miya-san was constantly talking about during one period of time. It was Iwanami Shinsho's *Saibai shokubutsu to noko no kigen* (Cultivated Plants and the Origins of Agriculture, 1966) by Sasuke Nakao. One day Miya-san asked me if I had read the book, and when I said I hadn't, he blurted out, "You ignoramus!" This book would later play a part in the thinking behind *Mononoke-hime* (Princess Mononoke; 1997). Incidentally, it was Takahata who introduced me to Noriko Ibaraki's excellent *Shi no kokoro o yomu* (Looking into the Heart of Poetry, Iwanami Junior Shinsho, 1979).

At any rate, the idea was to read all the books they read, to work my way through them whether I understood them or not. So whenever I got the opportunity, I would ask what they were reading, and then read the same books myself. I did this over and over again.

### "Uh-huh," "I See": The Art of Interjections

I often mention the importance of interjecting a comment now and then to keep a conversation going smoothly. I think this habit has something to do with my experience at this time. Interjections are, after all, a sign that one is intellectually in sync with the person one is conversing with.

Some people are in the habit of repeatedly saying, "Oh, really?" That kind of interjection just won't do. If you know the other party, have studied up on him or her, there must be something else you can say. Some individuals are in the habit of employing interjections to indicate they understand when they actually don't. This kind of interjection is just a sign of weakness. If you don't understand, ask for clarification. That is what I invariably tell new employees at Ghibli.

When the matter of interjections is brought up, some people may think the subject is trivial and mundane, but that is not the case. In fact, when I was asked to lecture as an adjunct professor at the University of Tokyo in the Content Creation and Management Course, Interfaculty Initiative in Information Studies, from 2004 to 2009, my topic was the art of interjections. Since it was a graduate school course, there were only about thirty students in attendance, all of whom seemed puzzled about the lecture's theme.

Let me be clear. When I say that the parties to a conversation must share an intellectual base, I am not referring simply to book learning. For example, Takahata and Miyazaki knew by heart every scene in the first part of NHK's TV series *The Silk Road*. When I was asked what I thought about it, I couldn't bring myself to give a noncommittal response. Since, in fact, I hadn't seen *The Silk Road* yet, I had to frantically catch up later on. In any case, it is my policy not to utter vapid interjections when I am unsure of myself. In order to interject a valid comment, there must be a shared intellectual base, a shared foundation, and shared data.

In hindsight, I think it was my effort to establish a relationship with Takahata and Miyazaki that led me to this way of thinking.

# 3 The Importance of Being the Director's Ally

## *Nausicaä of the Valley of the Wind* and the Founding of Studio Ghibli

前略
「風の谷のナウシカ」以来、「アニメージュ」の編集とアニメーション
映画の製作という二足のわらじをはいて参りま
したが、諸先輩の勧めもあり、この度、アニメーション
の仕事に専念することにあいなりました。
人並みに色々悩みもしましたが、そんな折、
ふと想い出したのが、高校時代に愛唱した
植木等の歌でした。
♪ 金の無い奴ァ　俺んとこへ来い
俺も無いけど　心配すんな
見ろよ　青い空　白い雲
そのうち　何とか　な～るだろう
ーてな具合いで、今後はスタジオ・ジブリで頑
張りますので、何卒、宜敷くお願い致します。

1989年9月末日

鈴木敏夫

The 1989 announcement sent by Toshio Suzuki to relevant parties, informing them that he had transferred from Tokuma Shoten to full-time work at Ghibli. He mentions the difficulty of making the decision, but recalls that a line from the comedian, actor, and singer Hitoshi Ueki's popular song always provided support: "Somehow things'll turn out fine."

**Isao Takahata**

---

Hayao Miyazaki is an incredibly hard worker. And according to him I am "descended from a giant sloth." Many good friends have helped me by prying my three toes from the tree branches to which they often cling, but among them Miya-san has always been special. And how has he helped? First, with his fierce dedication to work and his boundless talents. Second, these qualities have themselves created a necessary but formidable tension and power. It is through Hayao Miyazaki's very existence that I have always felt scolded for my slothlike tendencies, been made to feel guilty, been cornered into doing work, and had something greater than whatever limited talents I might possess squeezed out of me. This was especially true in our younger days when—had I not had the opportunity to witness his selfless devotion to work—I probably would only have done compromised, mediocre work.

("The Fireworks of Eros," *Starting Point: 1979–1996*, Hayao Miyazaki; trans. Beth Cary and Frederik L. Schodt, 1996)

---

## From a Dead Project Emerges the Manga *Nausicaä*

After getting on friendly terms with Miyazaki and Takahata, and with *Animage* proceeding smoothly, I got a little greedy and ambitious, wanting to try this and that. At the time, the president of Tokuma Shoten, Yasuyoshi Tokuma, was trying to create a medium that mixed film, music, and publication. He constantly said, "If you have a good idea, bring it to me."

It was in 1981 when I made my first proposal. My thinking during this period is recorded in my 2005 book *Eiga doraku* (Mixing Film with Pleasure), so I will quote it here.

> *Based on my thinking that animation was one of the genres in film, I discussed the subject with Miyazaki and presented some proposals. The first proposal was for a swashbuckling samurai piece* [chanbara mono] *tentatively titled* Sengoku majo *(Magic Civil War Castle). When Miyazaki makes something, various images tend to overlap, such as the legends of Jutaro Iwami's subjugation of an evil baboon and Tota Tawara's conquering of a giant centipede. I wanted to make something like that. It wasn't just that these legends were interesting in themselves, but that there was something quintessentially Japanese about them in the weak overcoming the strong. Since the words "magic castle" appeared in the title, there would, naturally, be a castle, but what he was striving for was the feel of a simpler version of* Princess Mononoke, *something that might, in fact, be considered its prototype.*

In the end the proposal got a no-go. The reason given was unbelievable. They said it wasn't based on an existing work! At the meeting were some people from the Tokuma group's film company, Daiei. They said that you could never have a hit with a film that wasn't based on an original work. When I told Miyazaki about it, he had a good answer. "Well, let's make an original work, then," he said. This marked the beginning of the serialization of *Nausicaä of the Valley of the Wind* in the February 1982 issue of *Animage*.

Before we could get started, though, something occurred that was very typical of Miyazaki. It had to do with the style of drawing. From the beginning we had decided that the story would be depicted on a grand, magnificent scale, but we hadn't decided on the drawing style. Then one day I got a call from Miyazaki. "I want to see you immediately," he said. Wondering what was up, I arrived to see the opening pages of *Nausicaä* drawn in three different ways. One was in the current meticulous style. The second was just the opposite, done without much detail or nuance. "In the style of Leiji Matsumoto," Miyazaki remarked. The third was something in between.

"Which do you like best?" he asked. It wasn't an easy question to answer.

According to Miyazaki, adopting the meticulous approach would mean he could only draw one page a day. With the less detailed format, he could do twenty-four pages. "Which shall it be?" he asked again. It was a difficult call; it wasn't as though you could weigh them on a scale. As I was pondering the matter, he couldn't help but press me for an answer. "Suzuki-san, what do you think?" If I chose the meticulous style, it could slow down the serialization in *Animage*—I realized this—but that was the style I decided on. I was strongly drawn by the unique touch and sheer density of the drawing. In fact, when *Nausicaä* was published, many people were not only enthralled by the world it depicted, but were stunned by the vibrancy of the artwork.

### The One Condition for Cinematizing a Manga

That was how the serialization got started, and it turned out to be another illustration of how serious Miya-san was about his work. We had begun with the idea of making an original manga that could serve as the basis for an animated film, but Miyazaki couldn't stop worrying. He told me, "You know, Suzuki-san, creating a manga just so we can base an animated film on it—isn't that an insult to the art of manga? It will be a failure; no one will read it. I've made up my mind. I'll do it as a full-fledged manga." This was very typical of Miya-san. When faced with a difficult choice, he always opted for the most honest approach.

But still, we wanted to make a movie. All my colleagues were in agreement. At that juncture Ogata suddenly said, "How about doing a five-minute pilot?" As for how we would actually make it, what form it would take—as usual, Ogata hadn't given these matters much thought. But everyone in the editorial department liked the idea, and the notion of making a film gained serious momentum. Ogata was great at evoking this kind of atmosphere. Before long the suggestion surfaced that we should present the pilot at the Tokuma Shoten–sponsored Anime Grand Prix, which had also been Ogata's brainchild. Ogata went to propose it to Miyazaki.

"I can't do anything in five minutes," Miyazaki told him.

"All we need is a little snippet, just a little feeling for the whole."

"But even then, I have to draw something that will hold up on its own, right?"

"Right. How about ten minutes, then?"

Out of the blue Ogata had doubled the time. At this juncture, though, no one knew how difficult this would be, and eventually the idea was put aside. After that, a lot of ideas were proposed, and it was finally decided to produce a feature film.

Miya-san, who hadn't been that enthusiastic about the idea at first, was finally swayed by the general mood and came around. But just as it seemed that everything had been decided, Miya-san said he had one condition. "I want Isao Takahata to act as producer," he quietly said.

At the time I didn't consider it of much importance. I just

thought, "Yeah, that makes sense." The two of them had worked in tandem on any number of animations; they were sort of like teammates. It was only natural, I thought, that Miyazaki would want to work with Takahata when undertaking a new project like this.

That's one thing about filmmaking. It is so much easier to work with staff that you are accustomed to; you don't have to worry about incidental details. That's the kind of environment you want. As it happened, just as we were preparing to get started on *Nausicaä*, Miyazaki had been out of work for various reasons, and hadn't been able to work with his customary staff. Takahata was a powerful force, and having him there at his side would make all the difference. "I understand," I thought, taking the situation at face value. I was delegated to visit Takahata and broach the subject.

It didn't turn out to be as simple as I had thought it would be.

## What Takahata and Miyazaki Were Aiming For

The relationship between Takahata and Miyazaki went back to their time at Toei Animation. Takahata entered Toei in 1959, Miyazaki in 1963—the last to be recruited through the company's regular employment process. At one time Takahata served as the vice president of the labor union, with Miyazaki acting as chief secretary. It was during this time that they made the animated film *The Little Norse Prince Valiant.*

Even after leaving Toei, they continued working together at other companies. At one point Miyazaki served under Takahata on TV animations like *Arupusu no shojo Haiji* (Heidi, A Girl of the Alps), *Haha o tazunete sanzen ri* (From the Apennines to the Andes), and *Akage no An* (Anne of Green Gables).

Miya-san's role at the time was layout drawing. In a live-action film this is the work that would be done by a cinematographer. It consisted of camera angles and framing.

It hardly needs saying that drawings are two-dimensional. One of the challenges that Takahata and Miyazaki took on was to bring depth to the world of animation. The two of them tried various devices to create the effect of movement from the foreground to the background, or from the background to the foreground.

This proved to be an extremely difficult undertaking, which you can appreciate if you look at classic Walt Disney animations. Basically, when moving a character, it was only possible to move it from right to left or from left to right. Disney never constructed a scene in which characters moved from front to back or back to front. With a 2D drawing it was very hard to produce such movement with a sense of reality. But this was exactly what Takahata wanted to do more than anything else. He wanted to do what Disney hadn't accomplished. Together with Miyazaki he studied this problem and experimented with it. It was an unprecedented endeavor.

Later on, as a matter of fact, their technical innovations came to the notice of Disney, which incorporated the techniques in its work. I discussed this in my 2002 essay "'Sen to Chihiro' wa Dizuni ni katta" ("Spirited Away" Beats Disney).

> *Disney in the 1990s under Jeffrey Katzenberg was very interesting, what with the rapid production of animations like* Beauty and the Beast, The Little Mermaid, *and* Aladdin. *One reason for this was that they were in tune with the times....*
>
> *Another reason Disney was so interesting during this period was the fact that it had studied Miyazaki's work. From the beginning it had been difficult for animation to depict vertical movement—movement from back to front. Walt Disney fully realized this, and up to that point Disney animations had only featured horizontal movement. It was Takahata and Miyazaki who tackled this problem. Disney learned from them, and its animations suddenly began to feature vertical movement. Viewing* The Hunchback of Notre

> Dame, *one can't help but notice how many scenes seem to be taken directly from* The Castle of Cagliostro. *[Laughs]*

Miyazaki's deepest desire was to be a lifelong animator. Even now he says quite seriously, "I am not really suited to be a director." If that's true, maybe I'm not suited to be a producer. But in any case, Miyazaki and Takahata had this kind of prehistory, so it was no surprise that Miyazaki's one condition for working on *Nausicaä* was that Takahata be the producer.

### What Makes Isao Takahata a Great Producer

I had learned how logical-minded Takahata could be from our first conversation over the phone, and my experience on this occasion reinforced that impression. Takahata simply refused to say "yes." After two weeks of my commuting to see him, in the end he showed me a notebook. He loved keeping handwritten notes—an onerous task in the days before word processors, which make revisions easy. In any case, he kept adding notes to what he had written, about producers he had worked with, the different types of Japanese producers, the contrast with American producers, the difference between European producers, and so on. And his interest didn't stop at film, but extended to drama.

Suddenly he said, "Look, Suzuki-san, I've just finished this notebook." Since he held it out to me, I had no choice but to flip through it. Near the end one line leaped into my eyes: "That's why producing doesn't suit me." I had spent two weeks with him, and this was the result. I felt my heart sink.

After returning to the studio I asked Miya-san again if Takahata had to be the producer. He was silent for a moment, and then said, "Let's go for a drink." He was perfectly aware that I didn't drink, and he himself rarely frequented bars. Still, that's what he suggested, so I agreed.

When we got to the bar, Miya-san started chugging Japanese sake like it was going out of style. I was taken aback. This was a side of Miyazaki I had never seen before. Naturally, he got drunk, and before I knew it, he was crying. The tears didn't stop. I was at a loss for what to do or say. He just sat there, drinking as if his life depended on it. Then out of his mouth came the word "I..." As I was wondering what would follow, he said, "I devoted my youth to Takahata, but he has never done anything for me." This was totally unexpected. I didn't know what to say, and didn't question him any further. "So that's how he feels," I thought. "Now I see."

Leaving the bar, I immediately went to see Takahata. "Takahata-san, you have to be the producer," I told him.

"No," he replied. "It's like I told you the other day. I'm not suited to being a producer."

My voice rising, I said, "Miya-san wants you to be the producer. He's asking that you be the producer. Are you refusing to help a friend in need?"

This was the first and only time (I think) that I ever raised my voice to Takahata. It was no longer a matter of logic. Finally he said, "Okay, alright. I understand." And that's how he became the producer for the film.

Once he had taken on the job, Takahata revealed his true power. In actuality, it is hard for a director to become a producer because of the sudden reversal of relative position and status. In any case, this was the first time for me to see how powerful Takahata could be as a producer. It started with his giving directions for the acquisition of a workplace and staff and continued with finding ways to reduce the load on Miyazaki. I couldn't help being impressed by the logical and sensible way he drew up a budget, for example. He determined how much each key drawing would cost, calculating everything meticulously and working out precise pricing. He computed the total incrementally and set standards for each area of work. This method was very easy to follow, and I learned a great deal from it.

What was particularly instructive for me was the fact that Takahata wasn't an experienced producer; this was a first-time effort. He was the type of person who returned to basic principles, who wasn't bound by custom or convention. He thought and studied as he went along, making things practical, easy, and comprehensible even for a novice. This was a great experience for me. I learned from Takahata what it meant to be a producer.

Later on I asked Takahata what a producer's most important role was. His answer was very clear. "That's simple," he said. "It is to be the director's ally." He meant by this that the director was in an isolated and remote position, and even though he might be supported by various staff, he was fighting a solitary battle. In the midst of all kinds of pressure, it was the producer's job to support the director of the film. This made perfect sense to me.

### What Can't Make the Deadline Can't Be Helped

Whenever the subject of *Nausicaä* comes up, there are always two anecdotes I like to relate.

One has to do with the time when production was nearing its final stages. As one might have expected, production work was taking much, much longer than we thought it would, and the film seemed like it would never be finished. Even the dauntless Miyazaki got a little flustered. Miyazaki is the type who likes, somehow or other, to meet deadlines. He called Takahata and me together with other principal members and complained, "As things are going now, we'll never make it."

Scheduling was the responsibility of the producer, Takahata. Miya-san said that he wanted to hear what the producer had to say. I still clearly remember what Takahata said, stepping unhurriedly forward.

"What can't make the deadline can't be helped."

At times like this, Takahata is not one to waste words. And his voice was huge. Human beings are interesting in that way: when faced with this kind of situation, most people don't know what to say. They just look down and keep their mouths shut. I myself didn't know what to do and just cast my eyes down. After a silence Miya-san said, "Well, if that's what the producer says, there is no longer a reason for this meeting." After that, Miya-san worked his tail off, burning the midnight oil. Somehow the film got finished.

Above I spoke about Takahata's greatness as a producer, but in essence he was a director through and through. As a director, his words, "What can't make the deadline can't be helped," had me crying in my beer any number of times.

I won't say that Takahata was totally oblivious to time management, but he was definitely not meticulous. There is this story about *Heidi*, for example. *Heidi* was to be broadcast once a week, so a stock of completed episodes was needed. The first episode was to be shown the following week, and everyone was working hard to meet the deadline. The problem was that the drawing for the opening scene was still undecided. Miya-san was in charge of drawing, and he urged Takahata to make a decision: "Paku-san [Miya-san's nickname for Takahata], make up your mind." But Takahata couldn't be budged. What with one thing and another, Takahata finally grabbed hold of the producer and began to debate the matter. I overheard Takahata asking, "Why do we have to do one episode a week, anyway?" They kept at it tooth and nail not just for one hour but for two and then three, seemingly without end. Staff can't do anything without instructions from the director, so there was nothing to do but wait. Left with no other option, it is said that Miya-san went ahead and created the opening scene without consulting Takahata. I have heard this story from Miya-san at least a million times. [Laughs]

Apparently this had been pretty much the case since Takahata's debut work, *The Little Norse Prince Valiant*. Takahata would take his own sweet time, and Miya-san would begin to worry. "Paku-san, is everything okay? At this rate we are not going to make it."

3月
4月

6 7 8 9 10 11 12 13 14 15 16 17 18 19 20 21 22 23 24 25 26 27 28 29 30 31 1 2 3 4 5 6 7 8 9 10 11 12 13

月 火 水 木 金 土 ㊐ 月 火 水 木 金 土 ㊐ 月 火 水 木 金 土 ㊐ 月 火 水 木 金 土 ㊐ 月 火 水 木 金 土 ㊐ 月 火 水 木

A 2/3パート・カッティング定尺 ↓ VTR

A 2/3 M確認打合せ①

A 2/3パート 作曲及び音楽録り

A 2/3パート 効果音作り

耳をすませば

A 1/3+Bパート・カッティング定尺 ↓ VTR

A 1/3+Bパート・M確認打合せ②

A 1/3+Bパート

4/1 PM7:30

音楽、効果、台詞仕込(スタジオ・ムーン)
MAC クワドラ950使用

㊙オール・ラッシュ

本篇

動画 3/15

動画CHECK 3末

背景

仕上 3末色指定

撮影

デジタル合成

OP&ED

※OP、EDとも本篇

タイトル発注

道川さん
※担当/川端

The hand-drawn schedule for *Mimi o sumaseba* (Whisper of the Heart, 1995), showing the complexity of the animation production process. The schedule has to be understood and managed by the producer in its entirety.

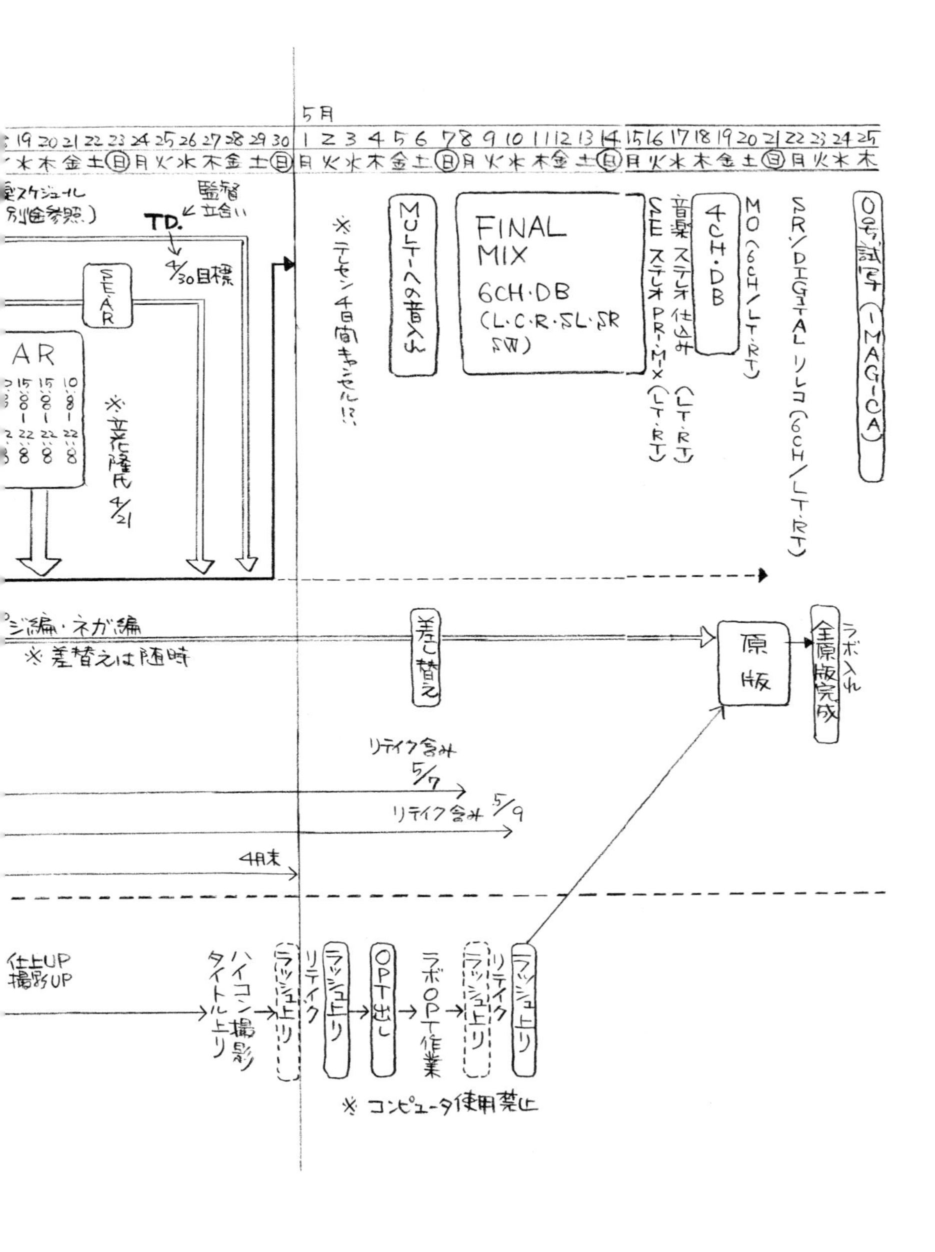
5月
監督立会い
TD.
4/30目標
SE・AR
AR
※テレセン4日間キャンセル!?
MULTIへの音入れ
FINAL MIX
6CH・DB
(L・C・R・SL・SR SW)
SE ステレオ PRI-MIX (LT・RT)
音楽ステレオ仕込み (LT・RT)
4CH・DB
MO (6CH/LT・RT)
SR/DIGITAL リレコ (6CH/LT・RT)
0号試写 (IMAGICA)
ジ編・ネガ編
※差替えは随時
差し替え
原版
全原版完成
ラボ入れ
リテイク含み 5/7
リテイク含み 5/9
4月末
仕上UP
撮影UP
ハイコン撮影 タイトル上り
ラッシュ上り
リテイク
ラッシュ上り
OPT出し
ラボOPT作業
ラッシュ上り
リテイク
ラッシュ上り
※コンピュータ使用禁止

To which Takahata would calmly reply, "Don't worry. I have a hostage."

"A hostage? What do you mean by that?"

"The film reels for the movie, that's what."

## Changing the Last Scene

Another anecdote concerns the last scene of *Nausicaä*. In the face of the onrushing Ohm, Nausicaä descends to confront them. At first Miya-san thought this would be the last scene. If this had turned out to be the case, what effect would it have had on the film? Wouldn't there have been a lack of catharsis, depriving the audience of a satisfying conclusion? Looking at the storyboards for the last scene, I had some doubts, and Takahata seemed to feel the same. We went to a coffee shop to discuss the matter.

"Suzuki-san, what do you think?"

"For a last scene," I said, "it's a bit of a letdown, isn't it?"

What was bothering Takahata was the fact that *Nausicaä* was meant to be an entertainment, and he was concerned that the ending didn't fit that description. Takahata being a very rational person, the conversation dragged on and on, eventually expanding to other topics. What with this, that, and the other thing, we talked for something like eight hours.

Then he said, "Suzuki-san, help me out on this," and we fell to considering various possibilities. We came up with three finales. The first was Miya-san's proposal, more or less as-is: Nausicaä descends to confront the onrushing Ohm, and then, suddenly, that's it—the End. This was very typical of Miya-san. The second, Takahata's idea, had the Ohm rushing forward and Nausicaä sent flying to her death, to live thereafter as a legendary hero. In the third option Nausicaä dies and is then reborn.

"What do you think, Suzuki-san? Which is the best?" Takahata asked.

"Nausicaä dying and then being reborn, for sure."

"Okay then, let's go and try to convince Miya-san."

So the two of us went off to see Miya-san. In situations like this Takahata could be very sneaky: he had me do all the talking. Why should he do that? Because he didn't want to take the responsibility. [Laughs] Even if Miya-san should agree with what Takahata decided, he might regret it later, and the responsibility would fall on Takahata's shoulders. Takahata didn't want that, which was why he wanted me to do the talking. I realized that, but it couldn't be helped, so I accepted the role of convincing Miya-san.

"Miya-san, this last scene, ending with Nausicaä descending to earth, don't you think the audience will find it a little difficult to understand? What if Nausicaä is sent flying, and just as you think she is dead, she returns to life?"

At that point the film was just about to be released, and Miya-san was eager to finish. After listening to my spiel, he said, "Okay, I understand. I'll do it that way." That's how the present last scene came about. For those viewers who were moved by this scene, I hate to divulge the real story, but this is the kind of discussion that goes on in the workplace.

Later on, this last scene would become somewhat controversial. Some complained that it was entirely different from the original manga, giving rise to all kinds of debate. Miya-san, being the serious person he is, continued to agonize about it. My heart pounded when he solemnly asked me one day, "Suzuki-san, do you really think that was the right thing to do?" Even today that scene bothers him.

This brings to mind the novelist Yoshie Hotta, who had written a piece to be included in the guidebook to Ghibli's *Tenku no shiro rapyuta* (Castle in the Sky). For reference I showed him a video of *Nausicaä*, and he watched it with great interest, which was quite gratifying. After watching the scene where Nausicaä is sent flying by the Ohm, he said, "Ah, that was interesting," and made ready to leave. I hurriedly told him, "There's still more." After he had seen the last scene I distinctly remember him saying, "Ah, so she comes back to life in the end, I see."

In any case, that is how *Nausicaä* was brought to completion, to be released in March 1984 by Toei; it drew some 915,000 viewers.

## One Word from Isao Takahata

After the release of *Nausicaä*, a certain incident occurred that concerned myself. It originated in something Takahata had said.

Just before and after the film was released, Tokuma Shoten published seven books related to the film. Among them was *Roman arubamu ekusutora Kaze no tani no Naushika* (Roman Album Extra: Nausicaä of the Valley of the Wind), which contained my interview with Takahata, the producer. When I asked him about the reason for the film's success, he offered the following analysis.

> *I don't know if Miya-san was aware of this or not—maybe he was totally unconscious of it—but* Nausicaä *is incidentally from the same mold as some of the most recent hits....*
>
> *Recent films have something religious or philosophical at their base. Even when they depict love or friendship, they must—or so it is thought—be a reflection of a religious or philosophical element.* Nausicaä *definitely has this element.*
>
> *From the viewers' perspective, there is an increasing desire to see something unprecedented, something they have never encountered before. In this respect, in showing something not simply from an alien world but something unimagined until then,* Nausicaä *is a rich trove, without rival.*
>
> *On the actual screen this is carried out by the density of the drawing and the film's compelling nature. The pacing is such that there is little time for the viewer to get bored. Meeting all these conditions, it would be strange indeed if* Nausicaä *were not a hit. I*

*think I can say, with a bit of exaggeration, that if a film like this was not a hit, what hope could any other movie have?*

Takahata told me to ask him how he graded the film as a producer and as a friend. So I asked him. He said that as a producer he gave it 100 percent, but as a friend only 30 percent. In Takahata's mind, Miya-san had succeeded in producing the film he was striving for (that's why 100 percent), but it was lacking in not having the present seen through the eyes of the future. Miya-san was not just an animator but a writer, Takahata said, and it had been Takahata's hope that the film would open up new horizons for Miyazaki. That is what resulted in this rather tough grading.

At the time I thought there was no need for Takahata to go to this extent, and as I expected, Miya-san exploded when he saw the article. "Why did you ever publish such a stupid book?" he said, and tore it apart right in front of me. Where did he get such phenomenal strength, I wondered; it was immensely impressive. Miya-san could not very well get angry at Takahata, so he directed it all at me, the creator of the book. I could understand his feelings and simply waited patiently for his anger to subside. But then something entirely unconnected popped into my head, and I said, "So you're really pleased by the reception the film has received?" He was momentarily stunned and suddenly grew quiet. Then he said, "So this is what you were thinking all along."

As a matter of fact, I was sure that *Nausicaä* would be well received, but one part of me thought it wouldn't be good for Miya-san to keep praising the film to the skies. Another part wanted Miya-san to continue producing more and more films, not to be satisfied with this success. That's what led me to suddenly speak of the film's reception.

To tell the truth, there were any number of times when I thought our relationship had come to an end, but somehow we managed to patch things over. This was the first of such encounters.

## The Founding of Studio Ghibli

Studio Ghibli was founded in June 1985, the year after *Nausicaä* was released. It was established because a production company for animations by Takahata and Miyazaki couldn't be found. It was widely known that while Takahata and Miyazaki could create wonderful films, the production work was immensely difficult. In fact, the company that had produced *Nausicaä*, Topcraft, subsequently went out of business.

Thus, despite the success *Nausicaä* had at the box office, there was no production company willing to take on the next film. This meant one thing: a new company had to be created. But, of course, I was a mere salaryman and had no idea how to set up a company. I went to talk to the director of general affairs at Tokuma Shoten, who told me, "If you're going to set up a company on your own, do the research on your own." After a while I was called in by the same director and informed that the president had told him to give us the use of a dormant company. As it turned out, though, this company was deep in debt; we had been given a white elephant. [Laughs]

At the beginning I was wearing two hats—one at *Animage* and the other in getting Ghibli underway. At Ghibli, however, I wasn't appointed to any official position. It was a very strange situation to be in, and I ended up making Ghibli business cards on my own.

Concerning the founding of Ghibli, this reminds me of the time I was scolded by the then president of Tokuma Shoten, Yasuyoshi Tokuma. The first Japanese animated feature, *Hakuja-den* (Panda and the Magic Serpent), was made by Toei Animation and released in 1958. The president of Toei, Hiroshi Okawa, had proclaimed that the company would become the "Disney of the Orient," stating that he would make an animated feature film every year for the next ten years. I mentioned this to the president of Tokuma Shoten, and said I didn't want to judge Ghibli on the basis of single successes but rather by where the company would be in ten years' time.

He immediately exclaimed, "Don't be an idiot! Done that way, if one film fails, you're finished." I was still young then, and I couldn't help thinking to myself that a real manager would include possible failures in his calculations. Even though I was pretty pissed off, still I could appreciate what he meant—that you should devote yourself wholeheartedly to the present project. It just wouldn't do to think that if one film failed, there was always a second or a third chance. That made sense to me.

## The Naming of Ghibli

Miya-san was the one who gave the name "Ghibli" to the studio. I have written about its intended meaning once before (*Sutajio Jiburi no junen* [Ten Years at Studio Ghibli]; 1995), so I will quote myself here.

> *"Ghibli" refers to a hot wind that blows in the Sahara Desert. During World War II this name was given to an Italian reconnaissance aircraft, a fact that Miya-san, as an airplane enthusiast, was quite familiar with. He chose it for the name of the studio because he hoped, as I recollect, that Ghibli would send a wind of change through the world of Japanese animation.*
>
> *Studio Ghibli was unique in Japan, and the world at large, for devoting itself principally to theatrical animated feature films. The risk attending original theatrical films was extraordinarily large. Conventional wisdom held that a steady income was more easily obtained by concentrating on TV animation.*

Incidentally, the Japanese pronunciation of the word *ghibli*, which is Italian in origin, was phonetically wrong; it should have been *giburi* instead of *jiburi*. It is a little too late to correct it now, though.

The first film to be graced with the Ghibli moniker was the 1986 *Castle in the Sky*. It drew 775,000 viewers. In 1988 there was the double feature *Tonari no totoro* (My Neighbor Totoro) and *Hotaru no haka* (Grave of the Fireflies), and in 1989 *Majo no takkyubin* (Kiki's Delivery Service). The latter was a huge success, attracting 2,640,000 viewers. In the fall of 1989 I became a full-time Ghibli employee, retiring officially from Tokuma Shoten the following year. The first film in which I was credited as the producer was *Omoide poroporo* (Only Yesterday) in 1991.

# 4 New Ideas Are Within a Radius of Three Meters

## Hayao Miyazaki's Filmmaking

2001, the Year of the Serpent. This is the New Year's card sent out by Ghibli announcing *Spirited Away* (to be released in July). It shows Suzuki haranguing the sixty-year-old Miyazaki, a director known for starting a film without a definite ending in mind, causing endless worries about the schedule. Miyazaki is saying, "I wish I were spirited away."

**Toshio Suzuki**

---

Miyazaki doesn't trust people who draw while consulting reference material. Instead, he says that anyone aspiring to be a professional animator should be curious about a variety of things and closely observe what is taking place around him on a daily basis.

It is this gradual accumulation that is important.

("Miyazaki Hayao no johogen" [The Resources of Hayao Miyazaki]; 2002)

When the castle in *Hauru no ugoku shiro* (Howl's Moving Castle) was made, he designed the upper part of the castle first and then various parts were added, the whole being made consistent in the end.

What we hadn't thought of was the interior of the castle. Only later did it become a serious problem. "What are we going to do about the interior?" [Laughs]

In the end, although the castle's facade was huge, the interior consisted of only two floors.

("Eiga o ai-suru futari kara no eiga seisaku no susume" [Advice on Filmmaking by Two Movie-Lovers], *Suzuki Toshio-Yamada Yoji taidan* [Conversations with Toshio Suzuki and Yoji Yamada]; 2004)

---

### The Overall Concept Emerges from the Tiniest Details

In making a film, Miyazaki's overall idea starts with the minutest details. How are the characters dressed? What are their hairstyles? What are they eating? What kind of houses are they living in? It is from these details that his image of the whole comes to life.

In 2004 I wrote a piece titled "Manga eiga to animeshon eiga" (Manga Films and Animation Films). At the time I naturally had Miyazaki's way of making films foremost in mind. The essay stated:

> *What one person conceives many people congregate to create. This, to my mind, is the outstanding characteristic of Japanese feature manga films. And this applies to even the smallest details. Which is to say, filmmaking starts with the minutest concrete details. For example, even before the plot has become clear, even before the script has been completed, thought is lavished on the clothes the hero will wear, on the hairdo of the heroine, and on the world they live in. These details and the script exercise a mutual influence. You could say that the theme of the film becomes apparent in the process of creation. That is why, in Japan, even if you hire a scriptwriter, it is largely wasted effort.*

Out of the blue Miya-san may ask, "Suzuki-san, what are we going to do with the heroine?" In this particular case he may be asking about her hairstyle: should it be in pigtails, bobbed, or simply long? Without knowing the plot of the story, how is one to answer? But in Miya-san's mind this is an important point, and he falls into a brown study over it. Later on, it may turn out that the heroine's hairstyle takes on special significance.

## Originality Takes Form from Memory

It is particularly characteristic of Miya-san that he doesn't make use of reference material when drawing. He creates something original by relying solely on knowledge of the past and memory. This can be seen in the Iron Town (Tataraba) scene of *Princess Mononoke*, in the bathhouse scene of *Sen to Chihiro no kamikakushi* (Spirited Away; 2001), and in the castle of *Hauru no ugoku shiro* (Howl's Moving Castle; 2004). They are often praised as depicting innovative architectural design, but in fact they emerged from Miya-san's way of working.

What is important to him is not the recording of facts but re-creation from memory. I recall the following incident. It was in 1988, more than twenty years ago, when Miya-san and I and a number of others went to the Aran Islands, located off the west coast of Ireland; they are famous for their Aran sweaters. The population totals only 800 people, and there is no means of local transportation. One night we were walking along a road on our way back from a bar, when our inn suddenly appeared in front of us. It was about ten o'clock, but it was June, when it's still light outside in Ireland. The inn, which I thought had nothing special to recommend it, looked surprisingly beautiful. Unusually for me, I pulled out my camera and took some pictures. That seemed to irritate Miya-san, who said, "Would you stop that? The sound of the shutter!" He was looking steadily at the inn, just gazing fixedly at it. I stood by his side, my eyes also on the inn. A jackdaw flew up into the air, further adding to the atmosphere. It was a special moment, indescribable in words. All the while, Miya-san just kept gazing at the inn without saying a word.

Shortly after returning to Japan we began work on *Kiki's Delivery Service*. In this movie there is a house where Kiki is supposed to deliver a toy resembling her cat Jiji. Miya-san was drawing this house, and when he had nearly completed it, he brought it over to show me, something he didn't usually do.

He asked, "Suzuki-san, do you remember this?"

"The inn in the Arans, right?"

"That's right. But there are some parts I can't quite recall."

Then he went on, "I think you took some photos." He compared his drawing with the photos and said, "Ah, I see."

When Miya-san looks at something, he looks at it seriously, intensely. He doesn't look casually. He grasps the object with all his senses, bringing to bear all past knowledge and experience. This was especially true of architectural design when traveling abroad. For example, in what century did a particular roof style originate? They were all different. With that kind of knowledge, looking at buildings became so much more interesting. Miya-san studied this kind of thing and committed to memory its different facets—the style of the roof, the floor plan, the windows. At first he would have ten or fifteen cases stored in his head, but with the passage of six months or so, he could clearly recall only seven or eight. A distinction developed between what he could remember distinctly and what he could not. What was vague in his mind he would leave to his imagination. Conversely, what had left the strongest impression on him would emerge and stand out. That's how his architectural constructions came to achieve uniqueness.

Relying on a photo simply produces a copy; relying on memory leads to originality. I myself have been influenced by this thinking and recently have refrained for the most part from carrying a camera. Just peering through a viewfinder doesn't produce a memory. It is far better to see with your own eyes and cherish what remains.

Miya-san would sometimes have fun by posing a query. Walking down a street, he would come across an interesting house and ask you, "What do you think the floor plan is like?" It is true, though, that in the case of *Howl* he only began to worry about the floor plan after the castle's exterior design had been finished.

His way of watching movies was much the same. I have written about this before in the previously mentioned "Miyazaki Hayao no johogen" (The Resources of Hayao Miyazaki), so I will quote myself here:

> *Sometimes, first thing in the morning, Miya-san would announce that he was going to see a movie. Returning to the office that night, he would give a report.*
>
> *"I saw five, but only one was interesting."*
>
> *His way of seeing a film meant that he didn't bother with their titles or schedules. If he went to Shinjuku, for example, he would pop into any theater he came across. Even if the movie had already started, that didn't bother him. If it wasn't interesting, he would immediately move on to the next theater. If the movie there was worth it, he would stay on to watch it. Even then, though, he wouldn't necessarily watch from the beginning. His criterion for what was interesting was a little different, as illustrated in the following incident.*
>
> *"I saw an interesting movie about Genghis Khan. I always wondered what kind of armor they wore in those days. Today I found out."*
>
> *"What was the movie about?"*
>
> *"Well, I couldn't really follow the story."*

In other words, his interest lay in what the armor was like, how people rode horses, and so on. That's why it didn't matter if he started watching the movie in the middle.

Another anecdote, this one about *The Castle of Cagliostro,* is slightly related. Not too long after the end of the war, work on the French classic animation *Le Roi et l'Oiseau* (The King and the Mockingbird) had begun, and later on there was much talk about its influence on Miyazaki. In his 2007 book *Manga eiga no kokorozashi* (The Aspirations of Manga Films), Takahata said (and I think he is probably right): "Even though Miyazaki hadn't seen this film that often, the fact that he was able to quickly adopt its effects into his own world is an amazing tribute to his powers of assimilation and visual memory."

### Being Inspired by Casual Conversation

Miya-san was fond of saying, "New ideas are within a radius of three meters." I imagine that almost everyone is interested in knowing the sources of his prolific inventiveness. In fact, there were only two. One was talking with friends; the other was casual conversations with staff.

Miya-san would say, "What is happening in Ghibli is happening in Tokyo. What is happening in Tokyo is happening throughout Japan. What is happening in Japan is probably happening throughout the world." That's why he asserted that new ideas could be found within a radius of three meters.

Take *Spirited Away*, for example. After the hubbub following the winning of the Oscar had settled down and things had returned to normal, Miya-san came up to me and said in an unusually subdued voice, "Your story about cabaret clubs was the starting point." I was nonplussed for a moment. "How's that?" I asked. I had completely forgotten about it, but I used to have a young acquaintance who was very fond of cabaret clubs, places where men can have a drink and chat with the club's hostesses. According to him, many of the young women who work in these clubs are actually rather shy, but in order to make a living they have to get used to talking with their male customers; in the process, they learn how to communicate with strangers. The same applies to the men, and so, in my friend's view, cabaret clubs could be regarded as a venue for learning communication skills. I thought this was an interesting take on these clubs and had related the story to Miya-san. He was now telling me that this was one of the motifs for *Spirited Away*.

It is true that the protagonist, Chihiro, is cast into an extraordinary world and is forced to communicate with those around her, and in the process her communication skills become much improved. On the other hand, the important character No Face runs wild because he is unable to communicate his feelings. He and Chihiro are exact opposites.

Miya-san had found the story about the cabaret clubs to be interesting and had put it to use as a core element in the film's broader image.

### Mixing with Staff

On almost a daily basis Miya-san can be seen making the rounds of the studio. If he is not sitting at his desk, he is most likely walking around. The studio is filled with different kinds of people. Counting the animators, background artists, and so on, there are at least a hundred people working on drawings alone. Miya-san drops by where they are working. There are a lot of things on their desks, not just the tools of their trade.

Maybe there's a manga magazine on someone's desk. Miya-san will pick it up and flip through it, with not so much as a by-your-leave, without acknowledging the person's existence. Then he asks, "Which have you read?" He knows that young people these days don't necessarily read all the serialized manga appearing in a magazine they've bought. "This one," the person says. "Is that so?" Miya-san responds, and stands there and reads the whole thing. Then he will ask questions like, "What did you find interesting about it?" After that, he goes on to the next desk.

Then there is the fact that many of them, particularly animators, work while listening to music. Since they are concentrating intensely on their work, they often don't notice when someone has come to their desk. Then Miya-san shows up and suddenly thrusts out his head, startling the animator. Miya-san has a rather large head in the first place, and up close you can tangibly feel his presence. Since it is none other than the great Hayao Miyazaki, the animator hurriedly removes his earphones. Again without a by-your-leave, Miya-san grabs the earphones and sticks them into his ears. After listening for a while, he asks, "What do you find good about this?"

This habit might appear to be an annoyance, but I think it has significance in several ways. Basically, there is Miya-san's desire to know what each man or woman is like. While this is probably true at the lowest level, doing it on a daily basis leads to an intimate knowledge of people's likes and dislikes, which eventually leads to this accumulated information becoming a part of him. This is undoubtedly what he means by "new ideas being within a three-meter radius."

As a matter of fact, most of the characters that appear in Miya-san's films have a model in real life. When a new person joins the studio or someone just comes to visit, if there is something unusual or interesting about them, Miya-san is immediately drawn to the person. He is a very curious man, and he likes human beings. He wants to know more about the new person, and he will go to be near him or her for no apparent reason. The desire to know more—that feeling is very strong in him.

Just recently this happened. We were working on *Ponyo on the Cliff by the Sea*, released in the summer of 2008. The protagonist is a five-year-old boy. Getting along in years, Miya-san didn't have any children of that age around him. Then one day Nobuko Shiraki, who was handling my scheduling, brought her child, a six-year-old boy, to the office. Miya-san immediately showed some interest. "Come over here," he said to the boy. "Let's play together." He had fun playing with the child, but he was also observing him. "So this is what six-year-olds are like now," he seemed to be saying.

He asked Shiraki when she would be bringing the boy in next. In the end she had to bring him in every Saturday, which I'm sure was not easy on her. One day the boy gave Miya-san a little present he had made himself, saying, "This is for playing with me." That really pleased Miya-san, because after all it's nice to be liked by children. This episode was eventually used in a film.

## Even without an Ending, the Key Animation Begins

One interesting thing about Miya-san's filmmaking is that he starts drawing the key animation even though the storyboards are incomplete; that is, the film still doesn't have an ending.

In filmmaking, the production is generally divided up into parts. One part is usually twenty minutes long: A part, B part, C part, each consists of about twenty minutes. This twenty-minute unit is the same for a TV series. A TV program lasting thirty minutes has only about twenty minutes of actual content. Miya-san and Takahata were old hands at this, so they took twenty minutes as a natural unit. When they had finished a unit, they started the drawing.

*Castle in the Sky* and *Kiki's Delivery Service* had a screenplay from the very beginning. The first film to start without a screenplay was *Porco Rosso*. We were behind schedule, and we knew the general story, so it was decided to begin the key animation. We told ourselves, "We can do the storyboards somewhere down the line." Halfway through, though, this procedure became firmly established, sort of putting the cart before the horse. Miya-san remarked, "It's no fun when everything has been worked out ahead of time, is it?" This became one of the techniques available in our arsenal.

The first time this technique was purposely used was in *Princess Mononoke*. Metaphorically speaking, making a film is like setting out on an ocean voyage: there are days when the weather is good, days when it rains, and days when it is stormy. The people aboard this intrepid vessel are the studio staff, and they don't know exactly where they will end up, how the story will conclude. The thrill and suspense they feel, from the director on down, is what makes the film interesting; it brings with it a kind of good luck. This was Miya-san's thinking on the matter.

No doubt about it, not clearly knowing the ending is definitely thrilling. Comparing it to a voyage over uncertain waters is a clever way of putting it, but following that metaphor, there is also the danger of shipwreck, of failing to complete the film.

*Howl's Moving Castle*, though very interesting to work on, had this very problem. The film was supposed to be 119 minutes long, but when the storyboards had reached about an hour and a half, there was still no ending in sight. Miya-san came to me looking very serious. He closed the door and said, "What are we going to do? How are we going to end it?" At times like this, Hayao Miyazaki has an almost endearing look about him. After hashing the matter out, it was finally decided, "This is it!" An ending of about ten minutes was finalized.

## Identifying with the Characters

As mentioned earlier, *Princess Mononoke* was the first film to be intentionally produced without a clear ending in mind. As it turned out, this put a tremendous amount of stress on Miya-san. Partway through, he became uneasy about the film's progress. I suggested, "Why don't you think of it as a serialized manga?" Serialized manga continue on and on without a clear ending in sight. This seemed to put him at ease. "A serialized manga ..." he said. "That sounds right."

But even then, the ending didn't come easily. At one point the film seemed just one step from completion, but I had the strong feeling that something was wrong. I told Miya-san what I thought: that the story couldn't be brought to a satisfactory conclusion without Lady Eboshi dying and Iron Town burning down. Even in historical chronicles, characters like Lady Eboshi usually die in the end. Moreover, believing that there was some truth to Lady Eboshi's way of thinking, Ashitaka would follow in her footsteps and go on to live with San (the self-dubbed Princess Mononoke). If this were done, I thought, the film would have a satisfying orthodox ending. Hearing this, Miya-san immediately responded, "So you were thinking the same way I was, Suzuki-san?"

The problem was that the schedule was so tight that if we included these episodes, not only would we run out of time but we would risk not meeting the release date. For me as the producer this was a huge gamble, but since my main task was to produce the best film possible, I resigned myself to a tough time ahead.

Miya-san agonized over this for the next three days, almost as if his life depended on it. The result was that Lady Eboshi would lose her right arm in the end; he couldn't bring himself to kill her. Invariably, Miya-san gets totally involved in the story and identifies with its characters. From the story's perspective Lady Eboshi had to die, but Miya-san couldn't bear the thought. To me he said, "Let me have it my way this time"—words I will never forget.

In his essay "The Fireworks of Eros," Takahata aptly describes Miya-san's tendency to identify with his characters.

> *The terrifying realism his characters possess is not the result of any calculated or objective observation. Even if he does incorporate his astute observations into his artwork, he remains possessed by, and fuses with, his characters—to the point where the heightened fireworks of Eros that result actually transform his ideals into flesh and blood.*
>
> *Miya-san therefore empathizes with each character designed to play a specific role in the overall drama, gives that character its appeal and its problems, and lets it have its say. And one result is that even his "bad guys" tend to suddenly stop being bad guys. Now, I realize this may be a tendency of all good authors who create characters of complex depth, or fascinating human portraits, but it may be amplified in Miya-san's case. He has to work with his characters for such a long time during production, and he can't stand the idea of creating any with whom he can't identify with emotionally.*

### Satsuki Won't Go Bad, Will She?

One incident that occurred during the production of *My Neighbor Totoro* typifies Miya-san to a T. As you may know, the story involves two sisters, Satsuki and Mei, who are the protagonists, as well as their mother, who is hospitalized. Satsuki is in the sixth grade and doing a wonderful job of acting as the mother of the family. Watching the storyboards develop, I began to think this odd.

After all, young children may try their best, but they tend not to be up to the task and inevitably fail in some way. This is what makes a child a child. I began to feel ill at ease with the fact that Satsuki was perfect in every way. I told Miya-san about my misgivings.

"This is a little unrealistic, isn't it? I don't think there is any child as perfect as this."

I should have stopped there, but still being young, I went on.

"If Satsuki is this perfect as a child, she's bound to go wrong when she grows up."

This really made Miyazaki mad. "No, there are children like that!" he said. "At least, there was one."

Just as I was wondering what he was getting at, he said, "That's the way I was." Miya-san had been one of several male children, and since his mother was sickly he took over the duties of preparing meals and other such things. It was this experience that led him to create an idealized character who superseded her own mother.

Miya-san got mad at the time, but he didn't entirely dismiss what I had said. He is the type who lends a sincere ear to people's comments. One day he called out to me, "Come here for a second," and I wondered what was up. It was the scene where Satsuki is weeping from fear that her mother is going to die. The storyboards for this scene had come up, and he asked me take to a look at them.

"Oh, so she's going to cry?" I remarked.

"I made her cry," he responded.

He went on. "So now she's not going to turn out bad, right?"

"No, she won't," I said, and Miya-san was quite pleased. Even though he was a grown man, he seemed like a kid. It struck me once again what a pure-hearted person he is.

### Memories of *My Neighbor Totoro*

I have so many memories connected with *Totoro* that I can't relate them all. Aside from the issue with Satsuki, in regard to the notion that the screenplay and the storyboards are equivalents, the first idea in *Totoro* was to have Totoro play an active part from beginning to end. It was an example of overexposure, I thought. As it happens, whenever I feel that something is off, I tend to be rather honest, and any doubts I have show on my face. Miya-san looked at me and said, "Suzuki-san, what's wrong?"

I replied, "Well, I don't think this kind of character usually appears in the first scene." I didn't have the nerve to say this was a case of overexposure.

"You don't think so?" he said. "Then what would you do?"

"Well," I said, "this kind of character usually appears somewhere around the middle." The words just popped out. I didn't have any solid evidence.

Miya-san fell into thought for a moment, but he didn't give in. "Why?" he asked.

"Well, in Spielberg's *E.T.*, the alien doesn't make an appearance until the middle of the film," I said, pushed for an answer.

"Hmm. That's true," he responded.

From this point on Miya-san showed his true mettle. He pulled out a large piece of paper and drew a line down the middle. On one half he wrote, "Totoro's appearance." He was surrounded by a large number of staff, all listening to the exchange. Without the slightest sign of embarrassment, he said, "So, the middle it is." This kind of alteration may seem a small thing, but it is not easily done. It shows what an extraordinary man Miya-san is.

Then he asked, "What is to come before that?"

"How about a raised finger like in *E.T.*, just a short shot?" I said. Let me repeat that I didn't have any particular rationale. I was just thinking of *E.T.* As a result, it was decided to have Totoro appear in the middle, but that meant we had to think of what to do with the preceding scenes. This resulted in the moving scene, the first day in the old house, and much more.

There are other anecdotes involving Miya-san, such as the following. Due to various circumstances it was decided to produce a double feature combining *Totoro* and Takahata's *Grave of the Fireflies*. Aside from the fact that this was a risky venture for Ghibli, it had the side effect of causing Miya-san to take note of the fact that Takahata's film was based on a literary work.

One day he said to me, "*Grave of the Fireflies* is based on a literary work, right?"

"Well, yes."

"I want to do the same!" he said.

"Uh, what do you mean?"

"Of course, we couldn't have anything like a Catbus in it, not in a serious work," he added.

I was absolutely stunned. He was going to cut not only the Catbus but also the flying top. "We can't have anything silly like a flying top," he commented.

I didn't know what to say. I really liked the Catbus scene, and without it what was he planning to do? I began to worry. I went to talk to Takahata, who was working on *Grave of the Fireflies*.

"Takahata-san, I'm really in a fix."

"What's the problem?" he asked.

"You know about the *Totoro* project, right?"

"I've heard of it."

"Now he's saying he will cut the Catbus and flying top scenes."

"That would be a pity," he said.

"Yes, a pity. That's what it would be, a pity and a waste."

So I went to see Miya-san. "About the Catbus and flying top scenes ..."

"What about them?" he said.

"Takahata-san says it would be a pity to cut them."

Miya-san always paid attention to what Takahata had to say. "Okay, I'll leave them in then," he eventually said, bringing the matter to a satisfactory conclusion.

## Nature as Depicted in *Totoro*

The person in charge of art direction for *Totoro* was Kazuo Oga, who was only in his thirties at the time. No one would deny that one of the most outstanding features of *Totoro* is the depiction of the natural setting of the villages and their adjacent forests (*satoyama*). Oga did a marvelous job. Looking at the background scenery, one almost unconsciously acquires a feeling for the transition of the seasons and the passage of time. Oga is a great craftsman. Just recently (June–September 2007) he held an exhibition centered on his work for Ghibli at the Museum of Contemporary Art Tokyo. The exhibition drew the largest crowd in the history of the museum. Of course, *Totoro* was not the only reason for this, but I imagine that many people were fans of "Totoro's forests."

Miya-san asked Oga to change only one thing: the color of the soil. The story takes place on the Kanto Plain, where the soil consists of red loam, but Oga had done it in black. There was a reason for this: Oga was from Akita, where the soil is typically black, an image deeply ingrained in his mind. So Miya-san asked him to do the soil in red, and I still have a clear memory of Oga intently working away, changing the colors.

This is how *Totoro* came to be finished, set in villages surrounded by cultivated woods. There is an interesting story connected to the film's preview showing, which concerned (*Animage* founding editor) Hideo Ogata's reaction. Miya-san was on pins and needles when the preview came to an end, wondering what people would say. Turning to Ogata, he asked, "What did you think?"

Ogata gave an indifferent reply: "At the end, during the closing credits, I thought the drawing of them all in the bath was well done."

Ordinarily this was the kind of response that would infuriate Miya-san, but Takahata stepped in and said, "Ogata-san grew up in such surroundings, and maybe the background art doesn't quite match his memories of life back then."

For Ogata, who had firsthand knowledge of nature in the countryside, the film didn't ring true. Leaving aside the question of village life, there was the issue of how realistically the surrounding thickets and forests were depicted. For starters, the woods were inhabited by all kinds of insects, and it was improbable that anyone would go out dressed in a short-sleeved shirt. No matter how hot it was, long-sleeved shirts and long pants were the required dress. *Totoro* didn't bring back memories of Ogata's youth. "I don't understand this movie," he said. Ogata was a very honest person. On the other hand, Miya-san felt envious of those raised in the country. The fact that he had grown up in Tokyo made him feel almost inferior. This led him to tease me about having spent my formative years in the city of Nagoya: "You're no good either, Suzuki-san. You're just a city kid."

Despite Takahata's earlier comments on *Totoro*, he later wrote in "The Fireworks of Eros" about the significance of the movie in a different way, which I think hit the nail on the head.

> *And speaking of benefits, I personally think the greatest benefit Hayao Miyazaki has bestowed upon us is Totoro, for Totoro is definitely not your ordinary celebrity-mascot character. Totoro's popularity has resulted in totoros not only in Tokorozawa, but in forests and woods throughout Japan. Totoro lives in the hearts of all children throughout Japan, and when they see trees now, they sense Totoro hidden in them. And this is a truly wonderful and indeed rare thing.*

On another occasion Takahata said, "*Totoro* is the apogee of what we are all striving for." Miya-san was tremendously pleased when he heard this.

### Not Seeking Reward Is the Greatest Reward

From the viewpoint of entertainment value and revenue, *Totoro* has something important to teach us. It began with the idea that it need not be profitable, but in the end it produced the greatest profit.

Miya-san has three fundamental principles of filmmaking that he is fond of repeating. First, the movie should be interesting; second, it should be worth the time and effort consumed in making it; and third, it should be financially rewarding.

Faced with a new staff, he would invariably repeat these axioms: that a movie should be entertaining, have a good theme, and, finally, it should make money, since they were engaged in a business. But in the case of *Totoro*, he broke these rules for the first and only time. To put it plainly, he thought that *Totoro* didn't have to be profitable.

What that meant is this. Compared with the directors in the old movie studios, the modern director has a tough row to hoe. If he messes up just once, he may never get another chance. So everything possible is done to please the movie's viewers. The stress is unimaginable. Even if the movie is a success in terms of content, its rating will drop if it does not succeed in drawing crowds. Fortunately, in this case *Totoro* was to be part of a double feature. The other film would be by Miyazaki's mentor and colleague Isao Takahata. Miya-san wouldn't have to bear the entire responsibility. That took some of the weight off his shoulders.

This is connected with the story I told earlier about delaying the appearance of Totoro until the middle of the film. When Miya-san agreed to this, he actually had something more to say. "Since it's going to be shown with *Grave of the Fireflies*, maybe that's okay, Suzuki-san," he had remarked.

In any case, there was the pressure of drawing a crowd and the fact that failure was unacceptable. This gave rise to the thought in Miya-san's mind that he should activate his most interesting character, Totoro, from the very beginning. That's precisely why he always had his protagonists play an active role throughout the film—as a means of keeping the audience entertained. This can be seen in *The Castle of Cagliostro* and *Nausicaä*, as well as *Castle in the Sky*. Now he was released from this stricture. It may seem contrary to actual fact, but *Totoro* contains much less gratuitous entertainment than most of Miya-san's films. It goes without saying, of course, that the movie was meant to be entertaining. For this reason—and I think this applies to all his work at Ghibli that I had a part in—there was never a film that Miya-san enjoyed making so much.

By way of illustration, there is an incident that reveals the atmosphere of the studio then. It had to do with Kazuo Oga.

> *When the director Miyazaki sets to work on the practical aspects of making a film, he usually wears a very stern expression, but in the case of* Totoro, *it was different. I recall his saying how easy it was on him that the film would be part of a double feature with* Grave of the Fireflies.
>
> *One day, when everyone was intently working on their drawings, and Miya-san was talking pleasantly with nearby staff while drawing himself, all of a sudden someone shouted out in a huge voice: "Keep quiet! Can't you keep quiet?"*
>
> *It was Oga. But after this outburst he continued on with his drawing as if nothing had happened. The air in the studio suddenly became tense. Everyone kept their head down, afraid to look up.*
>
> *After a moment or two Miya-san quietly stood up. With a piece of chalk in his hand, he drew a circle around Oga's desk. This was sacred territory, he seemed to be saying. Then he put a finger to his lips and, for all the world like a little boy playing at trick, he shushed everyone and looked at me.*

The fact is, this was the first time for Oga to take part in a Ghibli film. It was understandable that he should be tense and shout like that. I could understand that feeling, and I could appreciate Miya-san's good humor in the way he handled the situation. Miya-san was having great fun working on the film, and it showed in his big-hearted behavior. He felt liberated.

Thus it was that *Totoro* came into being, subsequently winning high praise and most of the film prizes for that year. The simultaneously released *Grave of the Fireflies* also won kudos as a film based on a literary work. However, due perhaps to the fact that they were released at an unconventional time, in mid-April, the box office was not at all good. In fact, out of all the Ghibli films, these two drew the fewest people. Since both films were rather subdued (having no battle scenes, for example), the distribution company was reluctant to take them on, and it was only after the president of Tokuma Shoten twisted some arms that the distribution problem was resolved. Against this background, it stood to reason that theater owners didn't have high hopes for the films.

It is here that the real success story of *Totoro* begins. In fact, the telecasting of the film was what caused its great success. It was shown on Nippon TV's *Friday Roadshow*, and the response was nothing less than astounding. This, in turn, resulted in an unexpected byproduct: the Totoro stuffed toy. Many people are under the mistaken impression that this toy was planned from the first, but that was not the case. The toy made its appearance following the film's telecast, about two years after its initial theatrical release.

Up to that point Ghibli hadn't given a thought to character toys. A certain person at a stuffed toy company was attracted by the possibilities of Totoro, and it was his enthusiasm that led to the toy. The licensing fees added considerably to Ghibli's bottom line. As a result, although *Totoro* had not been a commercial success when it was released, it was now the studio's biggest revenue earner. It's a bit mystifying, the thought that all you have to do is produce something of quality to achieve success.

Thereafter, Ghibli went on to establish a division to manage character toy development. But there was an inviolable rule that the film always came first, the toys second. The film should never be altered in any way in order to accommodate toy development. I still strongly believe in that.

### New Challenges and a Summing-Up

*Princess Mononoke* was completed in 1997, when Miya-san was in his mid-fifties. I stood by his side when he was working on the storyboards for the film, and I could hardly believe my eyes. Even though he was getting up in years, he worked with all the energy and freshness of a director new to the job. It was an astounding sight.

First of all, he had given up all his favorite techniques. To give an example, no characters fly through the air in this film. Typically, when Miya-san introduces new characters, he immediately has them flying around. In *Princess Mononoke*, though, there is not a single flying scene. To put it in another way, he had given up a time-trusted technique and decided to try something new and challenging, not relying on past successes. It was this air of openness and freshness that made him appear to be a director new to the job.

It was the same with his handling of themes. He would set up a difficult, seemingly irresolvable theme and then attack it as best he could. Sometimes things would get rather messy, but his youthful spirit seemed undaunted.

In the promo, when the theme was still unclear, the film was often described as "the culmination of Miyazaki's oeuvre." But that wasn't it. It wasn't a culmination; it was a new challenge. In this respect, Takahata, as usual, hit the nail on the head. At the preview screening of the film, he said, "This is not a culmination of Miyazaki's work; it is not a summing-up. Miya-san is still young in spirit. He has been reborn."

During the production of the film Miya-san would often ask me, "Suzuki-san, what do you think?" What bothered me, in fact, was the historical setting. The story was supposed to be taking place in the Muromachi period around the fifteenth century, but there seemed to be some factual distortions. Even in that period, forests that had been clear-cut would naturally start to grow again and not remain bare as they did in the film, and the fact that all the people working in the mining camp are women is surely wrong. That was my instinctive feeling, and so I suggested, "Wouldn't it be better if the story took place in a fantasy world?" He immediately replied, "Okay. Let's do that." This was one of the great things about Miya-san. He accepted suggestions without the slightest qualm.

Though I had made the suggestion myself, I had my doubts. We had reached the stage where we had to think about advertising, and I was worried that without a Japanese theme the film would lose its draw. After racking my brains over the matter, I finally decided that a Japanese background was best, after all. Miya-san at once agreed. In fact, though, even today I wonder if that was the right choice. I am still not sure.

One thing that I adamantly insisted on was the title. Just before the advertising was to get underway, Miya-san came and said he wanted to change it. He wanted the title to be *Ashitaka sekki* (Ashitaka's Mouth-to-Ear Record). The word *sekki* was his own coinage. It was supposed to mean a tale that passed from ear to ear. At times like this Miya-san could be very stubborn. "Everyone has agreed that this title is the best," he argued passionately. I wondered who this "everyone" referred to, but I realized it was just one of Miya-san's characteristic means of argument. At any rate, I was confident that compelling ad copy could be created with the title "Princess Mononoke," and though I was a little put out, I didn't give in. There was no eventual meeting of minds, and in the end I had to resort to brute force. Miya-san had no interest in special promos or trailers, and so when Nippon TV broadcast the first of its special promos (page 89, bottom right), I gave the title as "Princess Mononoke." I have written elsewhere about Miya-san's reaction ("'Mononoke-hime' to iu taitoru" [The Title "Princess Mononoke"]), which I will quote here.

> *Miya-san learned about the title after New Year's. He came rushing over and asked, "Suzuki-san, did you announce the title as 'Princess Mononoke'?"*
>
> *Slowly raising my head from my work, in an unconcerned voice I said, "Why, yes, I did."*
>
> *Looking rather disgusted, Miya-san returned to his desk. He never spoke of the matter again.*
>
> *This showed one aspect of Miya-san's personality, which depended on time and place. For me it was a huge gamble. During the advertising campaign, whenever a question concerning the title came up, Miya-san would invariably say, "Please ask the producer about that."*

Whether or not to forcefully create a fait accompli truly depends on the situation. I believed that *Princess Mononoke* was by far the best title and that Miya-san would eventually come around. I was taking a risk.

As for the grand summing-up of Miya-san's work, that would be *Spirited Away*. There he brought into play all that he had previously learned. All his characters are flying freely through the air. In that sense, *Princess Mononoke* and *Spirited Away* were tremendously interesting films to work on.

With *Spirited Away*, everything was going well until the scene where Chihiro, deprived of her name, is working in the bathhouse. The problem was what to do after that. Should we go with No Face or should we turn it into a story based on action and adventure? When

Miya-san asked my opinion, I was stumped for a moment. "Well, overall," I said, "an action-adventure film would probably have a longer life and be relatively uncontroversial. On the other hand, if we go with No Face, some viewers are likely to be sucked into his world. Will this create a greater draw, I wonder." I ended by saying, "Let's go with No Face."

Described in this way, it may seem that this discussion was long and drawn-out, but actually it was over in an instant. Whenever Miya-san asked, "What do you think?" he expected an immediate answer.

That reminds me of the critic Shuichi Kato, who, after seeing *Spirited Away*, laughingly said, "Japan has a lot of gods, so it's not easy, is it."

At any rate, Miya-san's way of arriving at quick decisions—you suggest that *Princess Mononoke* should not be set in Japan, and he immediately agrees, or you suggest going with No Face, and he immediately assents—is enough to send a chill down your spine. You want to say, "Hold on. This is an important decision." [Laughs]

## Depicting Women and Love

Next I would like to say something about the special qualities and characteristics of Miya-san's films.

First of all is his depiction of women. I have already mentioned that the workers at Iron Town in *Princess Mononoke* were all women. The status of women in Miya-san's films is a matter of some interest. Ultimately, he can be called a feminist, someone who values the role of women highly. His family consisted of his mother and her four sons, which may in part account for this perspective. He has a tendency to idealize women.

Historically speaking, it is not true that only women worked at mining camps like Iron Town. Miya-san was aware of this, but he wanted to think that it wasn't impossible. That society couldn't sus-

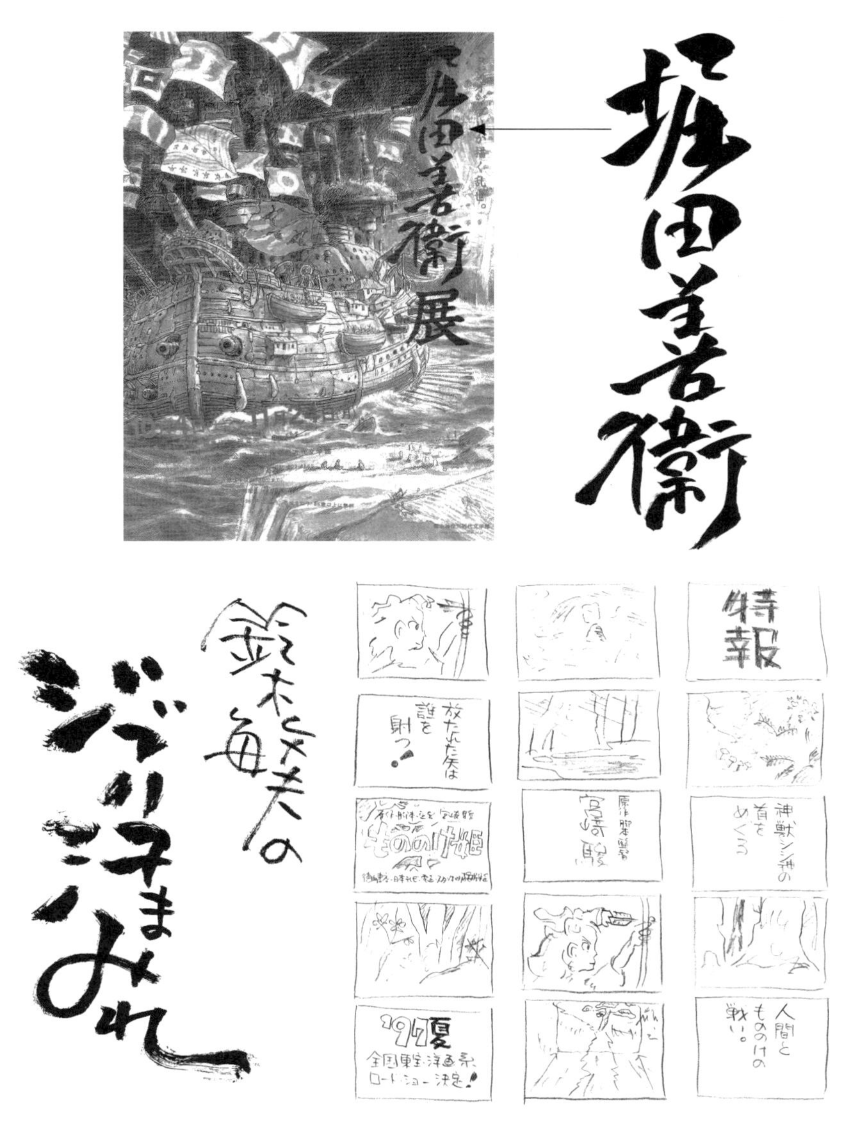


Suzuki made it part of his job as producer to draw illustrations and pen calligraphy. Above left is a flyer for an exhibition by the novelist and critic Yoshie Hotta. Above right is Toshio Suzuki's calligraphy giving the novelist's name. Below right is the 1995 special promo storyboards for *Princess Mononoke* that was broadcast after the showing of *My Neighbor Totoro* on Nippon TV. This was the first time for the title "Princess Mononoke" to be publicized. Below left is Suzuki's handwritten name (right) and the logo (left) for his radio program *Jiburi asemamire* (Sweating It Out at Ghibli).

tain itself without the power of women was something he knew even from the studio. Many of the animators were women, and it was women who worked their fingers to the bone to ensure the animation was completed. This thinking was part and parcel of his being.

When *Porco Rosso* was being made, the production happened to overlap with the film preceding it, Takahata's *Only Yesterday*. All principal staff were directed to work on Takahata's project, and to address his lack of staff, Miya-san made an unexpected move. It is hard to explain exactly, but in effect what he did was appoint women to all the key posts in the production process, women who were capable but had not yet reached the top echelon, and who were serious and sincere concerning their work. His catchphrase was "*Porco Rosso,* Made by Women."

Most likely, in Miya-san's heart of hearts was the belief that only women could be relied on in the end. In actual fact, this was already true at the time of *Nausicaä*. I have written about this previously, and although it is an internal document ("'Mimi o sumaseba' no senden o kangaeru ni atatte–aruiwa, kono nijunen no josei no chii ni tsuite" [Thinking about the Advertising for "Whisper of the Heart," or the Status of Women in the Last Twenty Years]), I would like quote a bit here.

> *The first film to go beyond reality and portray the equality of the sexes, or rather, more boldly, to depict the superiority of women over men, was none other than* Nausicaä, *to my way of thinking. After all,* Nausicaä *is the story of a young girl who sets out on her own to save a world that men have fought over and reduced to rack and ruin. In a sense,* Nausicaä *can be interpreted as a tale of vengeance directed at men. As to why the movie was a hit, critics have emphasized the conflict between nature and human beings. However, the film can also be viewed in terms of this vivid, heroic character who foretells a new era in human history. She awoke women from their sleep and roused their awareness.*

Postmortem analysis can lead to all kinds of forced interpretations, so one has to be careful, but in the case of Ghibli's work—or more specifically that of Miyazaki—I think that all kinds of interesting things might come to light if examined from a female point of view. His handling of the relations between the sexes is particularly noteworthy. The usual pattern is for there to be a fateful meeting of the two characters and then the eventual realization of special feelings between them. In Miya-san's case, however, it is 100 percent love at first sight. And in all of his movies there is immediately some kind of physical contact. When Howl first appears, he immediately puts his arm around Sophie's shoulders (*Howl's Moving Castle*); Haku wraps his arms around Chihiro and comforts her (*Spirited Away*). In *Castle in the Sky*, when Sheeta falls from the sky, Pazu is there to catch her, and the two sit in a small airship, shoulder to shoulder. Miya-san is very good at this type of scene.

Let me say a little more about love relationships. *Whisper of the Heart* is a love story involving two middle-school students. The boy, Seiji, leaves for a period of training abroad, and the girl begins to write a story. Ordinarily you would expect her to show the finished story to Seiji, but by that time Seiji is no longer there. What should she do? She shows it, as we know, to the older Nishi. After reading it, he goes into the backroom and reappears with some rocks. He tells her, more or less, that she herself is a diamond in the rough. In the ordinary world this would be seen as his making a pass at her, but he ends up telling her a rambling story about a girl he knew in Germany as they eat udon noodles. This is a romantic scene if I ever saw one! Who was the model for Nishi, I wondered. When I asked Miya-san about it, he got terribly embarrassed and laughed: "You have to realize, Suzuki-san, that Nishi possesses a lot of diamonds in the rough." Who knows; maybe this is one of the reasons for the film's success.

## Sensuality Built on Human Trust

According to Takahata, one of the most attractive features of Miyazaki's films is their sensuality. After serving as the producer for *Nausicaä* and then *Castle in the Sky* Takahata had the following to say about the latter ("Gendai-jin zentai e no yuai no monogatari" [A Tale of Fellow Feeling for Modern Man]; 1985).

> *To make modern youngsters, who only know how to chuckle, laugh from the bottom of their hearts; to keep them in breathless suspense; to have them identify heart and soul with the protagonist; and then to see them stride boldly out of the theater as if they themselves were heroes—this has been the aspiration of all filmmakers....*
>
> *In recent years, apart from claims in advertising copy, how often has animation produced "a fantastic and stirring adventure drama imbued with human warmth"? Even in the case of most mecha SF, which are intended to be entertaining adventure stories, human beings are depicted as feeble creatures in the face of the almost magical powers of the giant mechanical machines that are the fruit of the human imagination. We manipulate them like a TV game, in an almost neurotic frenzy; there is virtually no "breathless suspense" in a sensual way.*
>
> *It has only been in* Mirai Shonen Konan *(The Future Boy Conan) and other works by Hayao Miyazaki that the thirst of viewers for human warmth has been quenched....*
>
> *Today, amid the valiant efforts of viewers of every age to accommodate themselves to the coldhearted digital era, the passionate belief of Miyazaki in the analog of every kind, and his efforts to recover the rights of the analog in his works, has produced in* Castle in the Sky *a tale of human warmth for the modern viewer; it is a gallant challenge to the present unfortunate situation in the realm of adventure drama.*

Given that *Nausicaä* dealt with problems concerning the global environment, the succeeding *Castle in the Sky* can be viewed as a return to the children's realm of old-fashioned fairytales. However, Takahata adamantly refutes this view, and leaves me with the distinct feeling that one of the most attractive features of Miyazaki's films is their sensuality as described above.

### The Genius of Not Immediately Resolving Puzzles

Another feature of Miya-san's filmmaking that reveals his greatness is the fact that he does not make use of puzzles. One example of this occurs at the beginning of *Princess Mononoke*. When a huge boar charges onto the scene, the villagers immediately call out, "Oh, the demon god!" How do they know this? The story of how the boar became a demon god is only explained later. At this point the villagers should be clueless, but nonetheless they call the boar a demon god.

The same applies to *Porco Rosso*. Just think of it: a man with a pig's head is walking down the street, but no one thinks it odd. There is no explanation whatsoever. Not a word is said about how the man came to be a pig. At the time I wrote some copy about "the tale of a man who had bewitched himself and become a pig." But Takahata wouldn't let that pass. "Where is this in the movie?" he chided me. "You have gone beyond simple advertising copy." I thought that something like this was needed to get people interested in the movie, but Takahata was right: there was nothing resembling this copy anywhere in the film.

One last thing, which is unrelated to solving puzzles but constitutes one of the bewitching attractions of Miyazaki's films, is the matter of how he handles the age of his characters. One typical example is Lupin III. I once discussed this matter with Takahata; i.e., how old do you think Lupin is? The interesting thing is that the answer depends entirely on the viewer. For small children he is about the age of an uncle; for preteens he is twenty; for twenty-year-olds he is in his thirties. Each generation sees him as being a little older than they are. Don't you think this is amazing, that Lupin's age should change according to the viewer?

For anyone doing a study of Miyazaki's films, points like this should be very intriguing, but in fact no one takes them up. What a waste of good material!

## A Lack of Respect Makes for a Good Working Relationship

Miya-san and I have been working together for something like thirty years, and we talk with each other on a near daily basis. While we have had our ups and downs, it is safe to say that we get along pretty well. Once Miya-san said something clever about why that should be.

One day several years ago he suddenly showed up in front of my desk. When Miya-san has a good idea, he can't keep it to himself but must immediately share it with the concerned party. He is that kind of person. This day he came hurrying over as usual. "Suzuki-san," he said as if to tease me, "guess what?"

Figuring it must be something very trivial, I said rather coldly, "And what would that be?"

Then he said, "Now I understand."

"Understand what?" I replied.

"I know the main reason why you and I and Takahata-san have gotten along so well over the years," he said.

"And what would that be?"

"It's because we don't respect one another."

Whenever Miya-san says something like this, his face assumes an endearing expression. "If we respected each other," he went on, "we couldn't work well together."

I completely agree. It is the freedom to criticize unreservedly that produces good work. There is no room for anything like "respect." "Respect" means to hold back, to be reserved in expressing one's opinion.

But the important point here is that what someone tells you has to be accepted at face value. If there are any feelings of distrust, the message will be warped. There has to be a relationship based on trust. That is, there must be trust but not necessarily respect.

As it happens, Miya-san would often come up with an idea that I would oppose. This happened all the time. Nobuko Shiraki, my assistant who I mentioned above in connection with *Ponyo*, once told me, "Suzuki-san, you're all wins and no losses against Miyazaki-san." Then she went on, "But Miyazaki is really something. Even though he never wins, he still keeps coming back undaunted. That is really something."

But there is an important precondition here, which is that both of us are very forgetful. Miya-san, in particular, is a past master of forgetfulness. That's why we can be blunt without fear of repercussions. If we remembered everything we disagreed about, we couldn't maintain the relationship we have. [Laughs]

# 5 Filmmaking Is Like Tumbling All Together Down a Slope

## The Philosophy and Practice of Isao Takahata

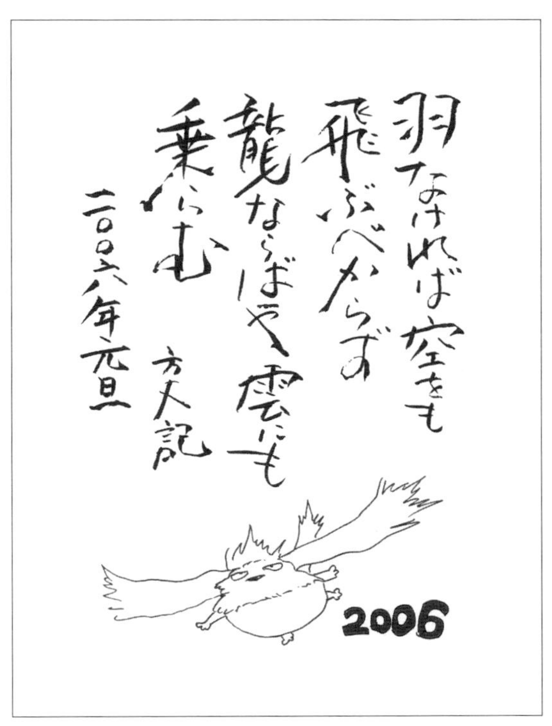


New Year's card for 2006, the year *Gedo senki* (Tales from Earthsea) by Goro Miyazaki was released, with drawing and calligraphy by Toshio Suzuki. The illustration recalls the scene from the film showing dragons flying in the sky. The calligraphy reads: "Without wings, you cannot fly in the sky. If you were a dragon, you could ride the clouds." (*Hojoki* [An Account of My Hut]; 1212)

**Isao Takahata**

What I intended in my work, including *Grave of the Fireflies* and *Only Yesterday*, was not, as I had until then, to have the audience become totally absorbed in the story, but rather to have them observe it from a certain distance. I have attempted not to get them to forget themselves entirely, but to leave some room for rational thought. I didn't want them to be frantically biting their fingernails, but rather by presenting an objective situation to keep them on the edge of their seats with anticipation. Sometimes I even want them to take a critical view of the protagonist. It was immediately after meeting Paul Grimault, when I was just starting to work on *Heisei tanuki gassen Ponpoko* [Pom Poko], that I began to work with this notion clearly in mind. The film was released in 1994, the year of Grimault's death.

(*Manga eiga no kokorozashi* [The Aspirations of Manga Films]; 2007)

## A Man of Principle

Whatever you might say about Takahata, he is unmistakably a man of unwavering principle. As an illustration of this fact, Takahata was never an official member of Studio Ghibli, which might surprise some people. When the studio was founded, he said that, without a doubt, the studio *should* be established. But in this case, "should" turned out to be a tricky word; he wasn't saying that he would officially take part in the undertaking. In fact, some are of the opinion that a film director *should not* be a member of any studio. He told me, "There is such a thing as a playwright in residence, right? That title would be fine with me."

So, on the day of the official signing ceremony, everyone was supposed to bring their personal seal, but of course Takahata didn't bring his. But not only that. To Miya-san, who had dutifully brought his, Takahata said, among other things, "A real creator shouldn't place his seal on a document like this." He might have been right, but he was also a mischief-maker. [Laughs] Thereafter, while he offered advice, he was not an official member of Ghibli.

Be that as it may, Takahata played a huge role when Ghibli was first set up. He was great at thinking things through, how to do what and when. That was a capability he had in spades.

I have already mentioned this, but Takahata's role as producer for *Nausicaä* was a marvel to behold. Everything he did was perfectly logical, including his accumulative approach to calculating the budget, which proved very helpful later on.

## The Pains Taken on One Scene

Despite Takahata's impressive experience as a producer, as a director he turned out to be a pain in the neck for all producers, exercising his perfectionist tendencies to the ultimate degree. The first time my name appeared in the credits as the producer was in the 1991 film *Only Yesterday*, when I was treated to more than a full taste of Takahata's perfectionism.

Two episodes come to mind that are very typical of Takahata in this respect. One concerns *Hyokkorihyotan-jima* (Pop-Up Gourd Island), Hisashi Inoue's NHK serialized puppet show, some of the songs from which made a small appearance in *Only Yesterday*. At the time Takahata had just started working for a living: he had no TV at home, and had never seen the program. It was then that a magazine ran a special on *Pop-Up Gourd Island*, giving the lyrics of the songs sung during the show. Two of them caught Takahata's attention. "I want to know more about these songs," he told me. The story starts from that point.

When a director says he wants to know more about something, it's the producer's job to track it down. I called an acquaintance at NHK and got the videotape for four episodes. Takahata watched them and found them "extremely interesting." He decided to use parts in his film, but the problem was that the two songs in question weren't included in the videotape.

Still, Takahata wanted to hear those songs. There was nothing to do but call NHK once more. Of this long series, only eight episodes had been captured on video. I got the remaining episodes, but the songs Takahata wanted weren't there either.

Takahata then asked, "Who released the soundtrack?" It turned out to have been Columbia, but when I asked, they said they had only released the theme song, nothing else. When Takahata heard this, he said, "The composer must have a recording. After all, it's his own composition." So I paid a visit to Seiichiro Uno's home in Meguro. He was a very nice person and tried to be of help, but he told me that he had composed so much music that it wasn't all neatly organized. In any case, he didn't recall the piece. Even his wife joined us in our search, but in the end it was all in vain.

It seemed that things like this simply weren't preserved for posterity. But Takahata refused to give up: "I want to hear those songs!" Just as I was racking my brains for what to do next, I ran into a rabid fan of this type of thing. I explained the situation and the dire straits I was in, and he sent out word to all kinds of obsessive fan groups throughout the country. It was about five days later, I think, that a recording was miraculously discovered.

The person who had the recording was living in Hokkaido. He sent the tape, and when I checked it out, the songs were there. Yet it all seemed very strange. NHK didn't have a copy; Columbia didn't have a copy; and neither did the original composer. Why on earth did a recording turn up in Hokkaido? It turned out that ten years ago a radio station had done a special on *Pop-Up Gourd Island*, and when the two songs were aired, the individual in Hokkaido had recorded them.

But the mystery still was not completely solved. Why had these two songs—nowhere to be found—been available for the radio broadcast? I asked my fanatical friend, and the mystery unraveled. It turned out that a girl named Chinatsu Nakayama dubbed the character known as Hakase (Doctor). She was still young, and apparently whenever a recording was made, her mother would invariably tape the songs that her daughter sang. It was these tapes that had been used for the radio broadcast.

Takahata was overjoyed. Having a good knowledge of music, he immediately created a score. "Huh, so this is how it goes," he said, completely satisfied. Ordinarily this would be the end of the story, everyone pleased as Punch. But not with Takahata. When I heard him say, "By the way . . ." I felt my heart sink. ". . . I wonder what the choreography was like." Since it was a puppet show, there naturally had to be choreography. Of course, we knew that there was no surviving video. "But there were puppeteers, right?" he said. So I hied myself off to Hitomi-za, which had been in charge of the puppeteering. It turned out that the person handling this particular puppet had already left the company. I talked to the former director, but not surprisingly he had no recollection. Still, making use of every available connection, I finally met the puppeteer who had left the company. He recalled the choreography, much to my relief. This enabled us, at long last, to complete this scene.

It was actually a very short scene, but it was highly lauded. Many said it reminded them of bygone years. It captured the air of the era.

## Compiling a Report on Safflowers

Here is another Takahata anecdote, this time concerning *Only Yesterday*.

The setting was to be Yamagata, and the theme the picking of safflowers. Since Takahata is the type of person who wants to know how everything is done, he was curious about how safflowers were grown, picked, and processed. Before anything else was done, he wanted to do some scenario scouting, he said. Since there was no turning him down, the two of us left for Yamagata. The prefectural tourist bureau introduced us to a farmer from whom we learned a great deal, recording everything on video.

While we were in Yamagata, Takahata had asked an assistant—and this is so typical—to collect all the books published in Japan about safflowers. After returning to Tokyo, he avidly read them all. Before long he had filled a notebook with annotations about safflowers. In effect, he had written an entire book on how safflowers are grown and processed.

In Yamagata we visited three farmhouses. According to Takahata, there was at least one more method of safflower processing that differed from these three farms. We later learned that there was a farmer in Yonezawa who was a master at the craft. Takahata said, "He must be the greatest of the great. I want to see him." We were in the midst of film production, and this idea wasn't even a good joke. I somehow persuaded him that he shouldn't go himself, and we sent a number of assistants instead. They showed the master craftsman Takahata's notebook, and he said, "Yes, this is the correct, orthodox way of doing it."

The whole procedure, from the picking of the flowers to their processing, it's all in the film. All the result of Takahata's research.

## Relentless Realism

Takahata was uncompromising when it came to realistic depiction, as can be seen in something as trivial as the bread in *Heidi, A Girl of the Alps*, which was minutely researched. Here is where Takahata and Miya-san parted ways. Miya-san, for his part, was good at making things *appear* to be real. For example, the Iron Town scene in *Princess Mononoke* appears to be real, but in fact it contains a number of factual fabrications. [Laughs] From Miya-san's point of view, Takahata's concern with realism was a sort of hobby; there was nothing particularly laudable about it. It was no different from his own interest in airplanes, Miya-san thought.

In any case, Takahata would do this kind of painstaking research for the sake of a single scene. I think he enjoyed it. True, keeping up with him was sometimes hard, but it is also true that the more you worked with him, the more interesting it became.

In the air-raid scene in *Grave of the Fireflies* Takahata became concerned about the direction the B-29s were coming from, and researched contemporary records. When Seita, the protagonist, looked up into the sky from his home, which direction were the bombers approaching from? That was the problem. I doubt that anyone who has seen the film has noticed the direction or bearing of the planes, but in fact it is all historically accurate.

This may be a digression, but the directions Takahata gave the animators were also very concrete and practical. He was never vague or abstract. He would never say, "In this situation this is the kind of feeling we want to create." Rather, he would say, "Make the character's eyes upturned here. Make the eyes rounded there." Those were the types of directions he gave. For Heidi, for example, he would say, "Make her eyes triangular." He knew full well what kind of effect this would produce, and it made the work of the animators that much easier.

### Anecdote from *Grave of the Fireflies*

Of all the Ghibli films there is only one that didn't meet its release date. That was *Grave of the Fireflies*. The circumstances are very painful to recall.

People who saw the film when it was first released will probably have noticed this: there was one uncompleted scene. Some people kindly attributed this fact to artistic effect, but actually it was simply incomplete. At the time this caused quite a stir.

As I mentioned earlier, *Grave of the Fireflies* was supposed to be released as a double feature with *My Neighbor Totoro*. Due to various circumstances, the project only became feasible with Shinchosha acting as the investing company. Progress was very slow. Since this was Shinchosha's first film, they began to worry whether it would meet its deadline.

One day a Shinchosha executive came to discuss the matter. "Since this is our first film, it would be scandalous if we didn't meet the release date. I would like to discuss this with Takahata-san. What should I do?" He wanted to know if I had any good ideas. On the one hand, I could appreciate Takahata's position, but I was somewhat obligated to the Shinchosha executive on the other. I didn't quite know what to do.

It was at this point that I recalled something Takahata often said. Given his interest in France, he may have been influenced by French thinking on this matter, but he often remarked, "A director can't give up of his own volition." The only time a director could give up was if he were fired by the producer. Only then would he acquiesce. That was Takahata's philosophy.

In the case of *Grave of the Fireflies*, the producer was the president of Shinchosha, the most authoritative person in the project. If he

1999. New Year's card showing Toshio Suzuki. He was in the midst of producing Isao Takahata's *Hohokekyo tonari no Yamada-kun* (My Neighbors the Yamadas; the film was to be released in July of that year). Suzuki is murmuring to himself, "To meet the release date or not to meet it, that is the question." The sketch of Suzuki is by the manga artist Hisaichi Ishii.

came humbly calling on Takahata, Takahata could hardly refuse. He would have to listen. Some ritual of this sort was called for; that was my advice. But no matter what, the president must not say that quality should be sacrificed; rather, he must say that quality should be maintained while the deadline is met. This was of utmost importance, I said, concluding my advice.

The morning of the fateful day Takahata seemed on edge. He said, "Suzuki-san, why don't you come along with me?"

"Don't be ridiculous," I replied, putting him off.

Actually, this kind of thing wasn't part of my job. Yet when it came time to go, I suddenly found myself conscripted. The person who would ordinarily have gone with Takahata gave me a deep bow and implored me to go in his place; relations between him and Takahata had become strained because of the delay in scheduling. The matter settled, Takahata told me that he was grateful.

It was then that I gave him a warning. "I am going today on behalf of the producer, who is burdened with a director who doesn't produce on time. Whatever happens, don't ask me to agree with anything you say. We are on opposite sides of the fence in this matter."

His response was: "What a coldhearted person you are!" I couldn't help but smile ironically.

We arrived at Shinchosha and were shown into the president's office, where the three of us engaged in small talk for a while. Then Takahata said, "I would like you to see what we've done so far, what kind of work we're doing. Then I would like you to extend the release date." That was the sum of what Takahata had to say. Given my role in the matter, the only thing I could do was to sit with my head hanging down.

The president responded by saying, "Takahata-san, please meet the deadline without lowering the quality." Takahata instantly replied, "Please extend the release date." The timing and rhythm were perfect. Given my position, I shouldn't say this, but I thought it was absolutely superlative.

In hindsight I feel bad about the president of Shinchosha, and I shouldn't be talking lightheartedly about something that should never have happened, but in situations like this Takahata was brilliant.

After that, it was decided that if the deadline couldn't be met, the release date would be extended.

## "Filmmaking Is Like Tumbling Down a Slope All Together"

Takahata is very fond of France. Since the French are said to be a very logical people, maybe he came under their influence; but in any case, he is a very logical person himself, or maybe one should say he is a past master of rationalization.

When *Grave of the Fireflies* was being made, I was working like a dog to see that it came out on schedule, looking for places to cut to save time. I mentioned this to Takahata. I knew it would rub him the wrong way, but it was a crisis, and so I made my case forcefully. He responded with an interesting but strange piece of logic. He said that filmmaking is like a group of people tumbling down a slope. The slope is the scenario. It has been approved by the producer; everyone has agreed to it. All the staff is tumbling down this hill together. The director is tumbling; the supervising animator is tumbling; the art director is tumbling. But they are all working toward the same goal. Everyone is pushed to the limit. In this kind of situation, can you possibly say to the person working intensely next to you, "How about making a change?"

I sort of understood what he was saying and sort of didn't; it was an odd piece of reasoning but very typical of Takahata. Everyone had agreed to the scenario, so even the director couldn't make changes of his own volition; it would go against the pact made with the staff. That's why there couldn't be any cuts. That's what he was attempting to say by means of an analogy. I wanted to ask him why, if he had time for coming up with an analogy like this, he didn't use that time to check a drawing or two. But Takahata was deadly serious.

Depending on the time and situation, Takahata would sometimes totally lose his temper. Not too long ago, a party of Tokuma Shoten executives showed up to urge him to meet the release date. Hideo Ogata joined in, saying, "The budget is at stake, Paku-san. Please do something."

Takahata became livid. He bellowed, "If you look at our plan, you should be able to figure out how much it will cost. But instead you use that as an excuse. What do you mean by that?"

Ogata tried to placate him: "Now, now, there's no reason to get hot under the collar." I was there at the time, so I vividly remember the look on Takahata's face. No matter how up in years he gets, he occasionally loses his temper, usually for reasons that are particularly his own.

## Arguing about Titles

Among the films that Takahata directed for Ghibli after *Grave of the Fireflies* (1988) and *Only Yesterday* (1991) was *Pom Poko* (1994).

From beginning to end, Miya-san opposed this title. Being a very serious person, he kept repeating that he couldn't understand why a film from Ghibli should have such a title.

The title was actually Takahata's idea, and he said in its defense: "It is not a stylish title, which is exactly the reason I chose it."

As it happens, Hisashi Inoue had written a novel with a raccoon (or more accurately, a raccoon dog) as a protagonist (*Fukko-ki* [The Belly Drum Chronicle]; 1985), which I had read and found quite interesting. I decided to ask for his help with *Pom Poko*, and he immediately assented. He and Takahata and I ended up spending three or four hours discussing raccoons. Inoue is really a great person, and he produced all kinds of interesting ideas. But Takahata turned them all down, one after another. I admit that it was all very interesting, but given that Inoue was going out of his way to be helpful, I couldn't help thinking that Takahata was really a terrible person.

Eventually, Miya-san and Inoue met for the first time, and they immediately hit it off when Inoue said, "The title of the film that Takahata-san is working on now, well, it's really not very good, is it?" There immediately arose a chorus of calls demanding that the title be changed. Ordinarily, if two people like Hayao Miyazaki and Hisashi Inoue were of the same opinion, there would be some second thoughts. As for myself, I considered it my job as producer to support Takahata. After all, it wasn't Miya-san's film. I wrote a letter to Inoue explaining my thinking, and he immediately wrote back, apologizing for sticking his nose where it didn't belong. He is really a great person.

I later wrote an internal memo on the impact of this title ("Botamochi-san Manpuku-ji hondo hameita no itazura" ["Graffiti on the Wooden Panels at the Main Hall of Botamochi-san Manpuku-ji"]; 1994).

*Everyone connected with this film has heard the title so often that they are no longer moved by it. But I would like you to recall the time when you first heard it. It seemed to be some kind of joke, as if you were being played with — it possessed that kind of impact.*

*In sheer power it was the equal of* Porco Rosso, *about which Shigesato Itoi remarked: "The title* Kurenai no buta *is great ad copy in and of itself."*

*The same thing can be said of* Pom Poko.

*It is the title of the film, not the story, that is counterintuitive.*

*Thus, if anything is to be shallow about the film, it should only be the title. The rest should be deadly serious—whether it's the drawing, the copy, or the sub-copy. If seriousness is stressed, the gap between the title and the content will grow even greater. On the other hand, if everything is treated with a lighthearted, fun-filled touch, the overall image of the film will shrink and be cheapened. There would be no difference between it and films for children shown at theaters, as represented by the* Toei Manga Matsuri *[Toei Manga Festival]. This is the scary part. To be a success a film must first appeal to adult audiences.*

In this memo I didn't describe the film as being a story of humanity's destruction of nature; neither did I say it was a story of raccoons versus human beings. I said that it was a tale of raccoons against raccoons—Japan's first "raccoon film," pure and simple. I considered it a film that broke the Ghibli standard—that is, the serious Miyazaki mold—and introduced a toxic element throughout.

In the end, *Pom Poko* became the top revenue earner among Japanese films that year. I was particularly pleased to learn that more than seventy percent of the audience were adults twenty years old or older.

Incidentally, in his book *Manga eiga no kokorozashi* (The Aspirations of Manga Films) Takahata wrote that he consciously strove to create films that weren't told exclusively from the protagonist's point of view, as touched upon in the excerpt at the beginning of this chapter. In his younger days he had been lured into the world of animation by his deep emotional response to *Le Roi et l'Oiseau* (The King and the Mockingbird) by Paul Grimault and Jacques Prévert. In that sense *Pom Poko* was a hugely important work for Takahata. Takahata presents a good contrast to Miya-san, who invariably tells the story from the protagonist's viewpoint.

## Takahata and Miyazaki in Comparison

The pairing of Takahata and Miyazaki presents an interesting combination.

Miya-san has only one viewer in mind when he makes a film; that person is Takahata. Miya-san himself often mentions this.

Even now Miya-san often goes up to the third floor at Ghibli and chats with the young staff there. But more than half of what he says has to do with Takahata. Once, speaking before a camera, he was asked if he ever dreamed. He replied, "I do. But only one person appears: Takahata-san." For Miya-san, Takahata was a lifelong influence.

Takahata was his senior, his rival, and sometimes almost a love-hate figure … Working on storyboards, even now he will say, "Doing it the way we are now, Suzuki-san, I'll get scolded by Paku-san." These are the words of a sixty-seven-year-old man! Still, I can't help feeling a little envious.

# 6 There Is No End to Worrying in This World

## The Life of Yasuyoshi Tokuma

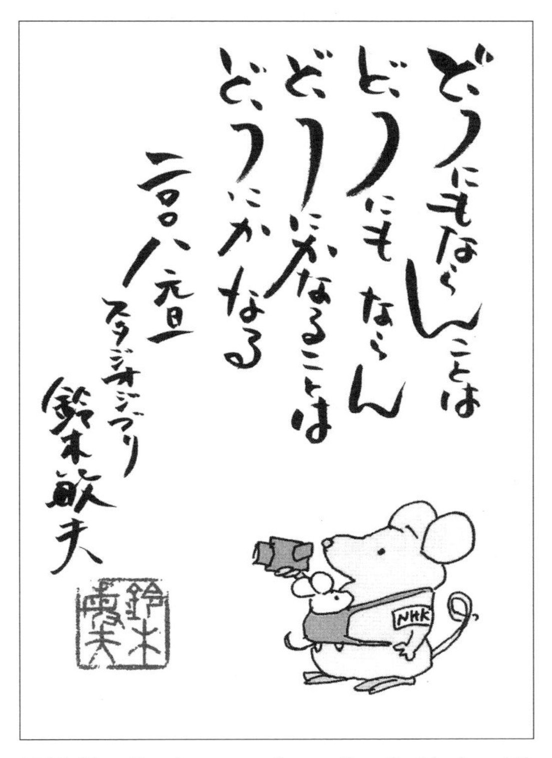


2008. New Year's postcard revealing Toshio Suzuki's state of mind while working on *Ponyo on the Cliff by the Sea*. The calligraphy reads, "What can't be done can't be done. What can be done, can."

**Toshio Suzuki**

---

Making movies for entertainment [*goraku eiga*] based on literary works—this was one of the primary activities that characterized Yasuyoshi Tokuma, president of Tokuma Shoten.

Take as examples *Tonko* [Dunhuang] and *Oroshiyakoku suimutan* [Dreams of Russia], both based on novels. Ordinarily, both of these would have become literary films [*bungei eiga*], but it is very characteristic of Yasuyoshi Tokuma that he turned them into entertainment films....

Immediately after the end of the war, Tokuma was forced to quit the *Yomiuri* newspaper as part of the so-called red purge. In 1948, at the invitation of Tatsuhiko Nakano, an old college friend of Tokuma's and the son of the politician and journalist Seigo Nakano, he joined the small publisher Shinzenbisha as a director. Shinzenbisha played a huge role in the publication of postwar literature and was an almost legendary presence.... Unfortunately, the books Shinzenbisha published were too sophisticated and didn't sell well.... In any case, after many a twist and turn, Tokuma's first success as a businessman would have to await the launching of the weekly magazine *Asahi Geino*.

What President Tokuma learned from this experience, I imagine, was that the general public sought not great literature but entertainment. This became his philosophy. Still, the dreams and aspirations of youth cannot be so easily abandoned. This dilemma was resolved by using literary works as the basis of entertainment films. This became, I think, the lifework of a man who was essentially an idealist at heart.

("Tokuma shacho to Noma Hiroshi" [President Tokuma and Hiroshi Noma]; 2001)

---

## "Money? It's Nothing but Paper"

I was tremendously influenced by Yasuyoshi Tokuma, former president of Tokuma Shoten. He was born in 1921 and died in the autumn of 2000. When Ghibli came into being, he was in his early sixties, the prime of his working life.

Whenever there was any uncertainty about whether to do something or not, he typically said, "Do it!" When I went to get his approval for setting up Ghibli, he was quick with a positive answer. Many a time he urged me on when I was hesitant. Around the time Ghibli was established I had more opportunities to talk to him directly. Somewhere along the line, he began to refer to me familiarly as "Toshio" or "Toshi-chan."

While it is true that I learned the ABC's of being a producer from Takahata, it is also true that I learned a great deal from Yasuyoshi Tokuma. I consider him a great producer. Basically, he left matters in the hands of the staff and was not often seen in the studio, only making an appearance at decisive moments. In his resolution of issues concerning the cinematization of *Nausicaä* and the establishment of Ghibli, as well as in the prowess he showed in negotiating problems concerning the distribution of *Totoro* and *Grave of the Fireflies*, we were in his debt. It is fair to say that without President Tokuma, Ghibli as we know it today would not exist.

That leaves the question of his abilities as a manager, as a businessman. The fact is, he borrowed money like it was going out of style and failed in one enterprise after another. His view of monetary matters was unique. I still remember one of his famous pronouncements: "Money? It's nothing but paper." At first, I wondered what he was talking about. But then I thought, yes, that's one way of looking at it, and I felt the burden on my shoulders become somewhat lighter.

The issue was how money was to be used. Tokuma's thinking was, "Money in banks does no one any good. I'll put it to use for them."

As an illustration of this attitude, he provided a good deal of financial assistance to rising Chinese directors. He advised them, "Show in your films how badly the Japanese army behaved in China." Given China's restrictive economic policy at the time, he was unable to provide any official financial support to Zhang Yimou's debut work, *Hong gaoliang* (Red Sorghum; 1987), but I understand that he did so unofficially. He openly supported Zhang's *Ju Dou* (Ju Dou; 1990). He saw to it that Tian Zhuangzhuang's *Lan fengzheng* (The Blue Kite; 1993), which depicted the Cultural Revolution, was entered in the Tokyo International Film Festival. He seemed to be having fun angering the Chinese government. He even went so far as to take care of the living expenses of the most dynamic directors. Even today many people are still grateful to President Tokuma for his kindness.

It was impossible for me to emulate President Tokuma, but being by his side I was bound to be influenced. At one point I was in charge of banking and had any number of opportunities to accompany him on visits to banks. Observed up close, his approach was really something to behold.

His personal axiom, as mentioned above, was, "Money? It's nothing but paper." Myself, being a somewhat timorous person, I have always thought it important to avoid debt, but who knows? Maybe that thinking should sometimes be turned on its head. Even in this, by giving my thinking broader scope, President Tokuma's influence was immense.

### "There Is No End to Worrying in This World"

One of the definitive turning points in Ghibli history was the construction of a new studio following the box office success of *Kiki's Delivery Service*. In 1990 Ghibli adopted the policy of putting all company employees on a fixed salary, in addition to periodically hiring and educating new personnel. It was in 1991 that Miya-san proposed that a new studio be built. This occurred just as *Only Yesterday* was entering its final stages and *Porco Rosso* had just been started. It was the first time that Ghibli had worked on two overlapping films at the same time, and things were terribly busy. Miya-san has this notion that the way to solve one enormous problem is to make it seem less significant by creating another problem of equal enormity. That is, he tries to nullify one difficulty with another.

Miya-san's reason for constructing a new studio was very clear. Even if we recruited and hired new people, without a fixed production base we couldn't expect the new employees to grow and thrive. A new building, he thought, was an absolute necessity.

But to me this went against all common sense. I secretly thought it absurd. Something should be done about it, I decided, and I went to see President Tokuma.

"President Tokuma!"

"What's up?" he said.

"For various reasons Miya-san says he wants to build a new studio."

"Oh, sounds good. Do it!" he replied.

"That's alright to say, but we need to buy the land and we don't have the money."

"Oh, money? The banks have plenty of that."

This is an exact record of what Tokuma said. The problem was that Ghibli wasn't in a position to be borrowing. Tokuma commented, "That bad, huh? Let's give it some thought." In the end we managed to scrape the funds together to build the studio. But still, the whole idea was nonsensical. The person running the studio then, Toru Hara, was flat against it and left the company, saying that he couldn't see the logic in it. After commenting that "banks have plenty of money," Tokuma went on to say, "There is no end to worrying in this world." I remember being strangely moved by this, an entirely new way of viewing life.

Incidentally, after the decision was made to build the studio, Miya-san went into overdrive. While working simultaneously on *Porco Rosso*, he drew up the studio floor plans, negotiated repeatedly with the construction company, and acquired and checked samples of the materials to be used. Particularly characteristic of Miya-san was the fact that, although the proportion of female to male employees was nearly equal, the women's restroom was about double in size. He also reduced the size of the parking lot and increased the area devoted to foliage. In every way the studio reflected his thinking.

### Oddly Childish

One of Yasuyoshi Tokuma's dreams was to cinematize literary works as entertainment films, as I mentioned earlier. The 1988 live-action *Tonko* (Dunhuang) was a blockbuster undertaking that required all his energy as producer. The same year also saw the release of *Totoro* and *Grave of the Fireflies*, which he also produced. As I said before, both of these films were having trouble with a reluctant distributor. Tokuma visited the distributor and declared, "If you don't do these two, I'll cancel *Tonko*." It was thanks to Tokuma that these two films were realized, and in that sense he was a true lifesaver. In fact, however, his real feelings lay with *Tonko*.

*Totoro* and *Grave of the Fireflies* were released in April, *Tonko* in June. As it happened, *Totoro* won all the film prizes, and *Grave of the Fireflies* earned kudos as a literary film. For Tokuma, however, it was *Tonko* that was important. He wanted it not only to be a commercial success, but also wanted it to gain critical acclaim. It was, moreover, based on one of the major works of the novelist Yasushi Inoue. Still, *Totoro* made off with most of the prizes. Tokuma must have had seriously mixed feelings about its success.

Maybe as a reflection of this, something rather amazing happened

Toshio Suzuki with Akiko Yano, the pop and jazz musician and singer, who did the voiceover for *Ponyo*. She had earlier provided her voice in the short *Yadosagashi* (House Hunting), which is shown exclusively at the Ghibli Museum. It is one of the jobs of a producer to find voice actors who perfectly match the image projected by the film.

concerning the release dates of *Porco Rosso* and the blockbuster literary film *Oroshiyakoku suimutan* (Dreams of Russia; 1992), which was to follow *Tonko*. Tokuma did the unthinkable by giving *Porco Rosso* and *Dreams of Russia* almost the same release date. The date for *Porco Rosso* was already fixed for July 18 and couldn't be moved, but then he intentionally set the release date for *Dreams of Russia* for just before that, on June 27. Ordinarily this would be unthinkable. Tokuma was the producer for both films and financing. He had a stake in seeing them both succeed, so it would have made sense to stagger the dates. Still, he set their release dates to be almost simultaneous, one following quickly after the other.

He seemed to be saying, "It's a battle! Who's going to come out on top?" Even though he was the president of the company, he was in effect challenging me, one of his employees, to a duel. It might be seen as unworthy of his position and status, but as one producer to another I could understand it. This kind of behavior could be called childish, and that might not be far from the truth.

## "Oh, So We're Competing"

Here I would like to say a little more about *Porco Rosso*.

It turned out that "It's a battle" applied not only to release dates. Tokuma was fond of these words in reference to almost anything. One day he told me that there was going to be an important meeting concerning *Dreams of Russia* and that I should attend. The production costs for the movie were going to be enormous, and the presidents of Dentsu, Daiei, and other investors would all be there. Tokuma started with a speech lasting more than thirty minutes about how the movie would change the history of Japanese cinema and so on. Immediately after concluding his speech, he suddenly called out, "Suzuki! What do you think of what I just said?" Sitting quietly in a corner of the room, I was momentarily caught off guard. Before I could utter a word, he continued: "Let me tell you what you're thinking. You're secretly hoping that this grand historical adventure story, *Dreams of Russia*, will flop as a feature film and that *Porco Rosso* will be a hit. Right?"

That was going a bit too far, I thought. We belonged to the same company, and he himself was also the producer of *Porco Rosso*. And all this was taking place at a conference with other company presidents in session. At a loss for words I replied, "Yes, it's just as you say." His response to this was, "Oh, so we're competing." To that, the only response I could manage was, "Pardon?"

Here's another interesting story. During a meeting at Nippon TV about *Porco Rosso*, a phone call came from Tokuma. There were about thirty people in attendance, including several Nippon TV executives. The person the call was intended for was reluctant to answer since he was in the middle of a formal conference, but he felt he had no choice since it was President Tokuma. "Yes, yes, I understand," he continually repeated, bowing into the phone. When I asked him afterward what the problem was, he said, "I have just been roundly scolded by President Tokuma." In effect, he had been told: "You spend all your time on *Porco Rosso* and do nothing for *Dreams of Russia*." Once you've gone this far, I thought, you can't be called a manager anymore. Still, it was immensely interesting.

The films were released, and *Porco Rosso* won hands down. Not long after the release dates—and I will never forget this—I got a call from Tokuma. The first words out of his mouth were: "You won! You must be so happy."

This time I couldn't bring myself to say that I was happy. This time I couldn't say, "Yes, it's just as you say"; it was just too rude. So I said something else, something that had been on my mind for quite a while. "The ads for *Dreams of Russia* have been all wrong," I told him. I summarized briefly what I meant. "You have to research what viewers found most interesting and use that in your advertising," I added.

Tokuma took it very well. He generously said, "You're probably right. I'll see what can be done."

### A Mind-boggling General Meeting

Of all Ghibli films, the one with the worst box office return was Takahata's *Hohokekyo tonari no Yamada-kun* (My Neighbors the Yamadas; 1999). It took in about 1.5 billion yen, which ordinarily would not have been bad. The problem was that expectations were so high that the impression persisted that it had done poorly.

Realistically speaking, *The Yamadas* was handicapped by the fact that Shochiku was the distributor. It hardly needs saying that one important factor in a film's success or failure is the capability of the distributor. Then, as now, the company with the greatest clout was Toho. Unfortunately, Tokuma had gotten into a fight with the pertinent party at Toho, so there was no choice but to go with Shochiku. Shochiku then was structurally weak, and most of its staff were new to the work. The theaters where the film would open were mostly in Kanto or northern Japan, with almost none in Osaka or further west. From a competitive point of view, this left us in an untenable position. We had basically lost the game before it started.

It was clear that the person responsible for this situation was President Tokuma and his stubborn insistence on having his own way. He realized this, and on the morning before the general meeting, he called me into his office.

"Toshi-chan, it's been hard getting *The Yamadas* into theaters," he said.

"I'm sorry about that," I replied.

"No, it's all my fault. If we had gone with Toho, things would have been different."

It was the custom at Tokuma Shoten to have a general meeting of all employees once a month. There were 200 or 300 people in all. The president would give a talk, of course, but other people were allowed to speak, too. The results for *The Yamadas* had already come in. Tokuma said, "Before the meeting I just wanted to say that I chose Shochiku and so the responsibility lies with me.... Well, the meeting is about to start. We should be going."

Entering the multipurpose hall, what was the first thing out of his mouth? "Up until now Ghibli has had one hit after another. *The Yamadas* is the first film to flop. The person solely responsible for this is … Suzuki!"

With Tokuma, you never know what he is going to do or say next, so I was usually not completely unprepared. But this time I was caught off guard, absolutely amazed. Since I would be speaking next, Tokuma added, "I look forward to hearing what Suzuki has to say about this." You could have knocked me over with a feather!

Still, Tokuma had carefully thought this out. First he calls me in before the meeting and says it was all his fault. Then, before leaving for the meeting, where we would be sitting next to each other, he cheerfully says, "Well, I'm off." Finally, at the meeting, he reprimands me in an unusually loud voice.

Now it was my turn to speak. I said, "I have just been reprimanded by the president. I accept everything he has said." Furthermore, "I have learned how important sales is, how essential it is to success. Just as with selling books, the distributor is a crucial issue. No matter how good your product may be, if the sales department is no good, the product won't sell. I have learned a lot from this experience." I didn't mention that it was President Tokuma who decided on the distributor. He would understand what I meant.

When I had finished speaking and stepped down from the dais, I saw Tokuma smiling broadly. He looked like a mischievous boy. He was no longer concerned with bygone incidents, but was having fun seeing what his people would say to extricate themselves from this kind of situation. He was a real trial.

This reminds me of an episode at a general meeting when we were working on *Nausicaä*. At the time there were a lot of intellectual and wheeler-dealer types at Tokuma Shoten. At the meeting Tokuma suddenly said, "Times have changed," and he selected Hideo Ogata for special praise. "Whatever Ogata touches, whether it's *Nausicaä* or anything else, it always goes well. I thought clever intellectual types were best suited to this business, but the era of the intellectual is over. Right, Ogata?" That pleased Ogata to no end, naive person that he is.

Looking back, Tokuma, Takahata, Miyazaki, and Ogata were all honest men who said what they meant, even if they were somewhat mischievous. And they were all "ideas" men. They had that in common.

### Backed by Fastidiousness

Yasuyoshi Tokuma might appear to be a bold, manly figure, but in fact he had a fastidious aspect to his character. First of all—and this is an area where he had an influence on me—he kept a diary with notes on everyone he met. He didn't do this halfheartedly either, but even recorded what they had talked about. So, meeting someone after some time had passed, he would start by saying, "Oh, about what we were discussing the other day …" That was bound to be a pleasant surprise for anyone, the fact that he remembered what they had said so long ago. This may have been the effect he was aiming for, and he never abandoned the practice.

In this regard, I had an interesting experience with Tokuma after the huge success of *Princess Mononoke*. The film was not only successful commercially, but had garnered much acclaim and received many awards. The awards were very welcome, of course, but the string of award ceremonies was very tiring. March, in particular, was a crowded month, and I began to wonder if there wasn't some way out.

Then, just as I was planning my escape from Japan, the TV program production company TV Man Union broached the idea of doing a documentary on Miya-san. Maybe this was my safe port in a storm, I thought. It was decided to do a program focusing on Miya-san as part of the series *Sekai: Wagakokoro no tabi* (Journey of the Heart). Our journey would follow the route taken by the writer and pioneering aviator Antoine de Saint-Exupéry when he was an airmail pilot, covering France, Spain, and North Africa.

What was so interesting about this trip? Well, there's nothing quite as exciting as riding in a biplane. The plane was an Antonov that was used for spraying insecticides. It was an old rattletrap, but still it could seat nine people. Miya-san wanted to view the landscape from 50 or 100 meters above the ground, and this plane was perfect for that. It had a top speed of about 200 kilometers per hour, and if a strong wind was blowing it would stall. We had no plans, no idea where we would stay the nights, but simply flew off in a carefree fashion. In Morocco we crossed the Atlas Mountains, having a great time. Miya-san said, "I have never had such a fun trip in my whole life."

In France we first went to Toulouse to visit one of the places where Saint-Exupéry usually stayed. It was there that we got a call from Tokuma.

"How's it going? Having a good time?" he asked.

"Everything is going very well," I said.

"That's good to hear. Very good to hear," he replied.

Next I told him, "I'll be out of contact for a few days." I thought it would sound convincing if I told him our schedule was uncertain because the plane tended to stall in strong winds. "Is that so?" he said. "In any case, have a good time."

The truth of the matter was that I knew that certain ceremonies and celebrations were planned for the coming days, and I wanted to make it clear that I couldn't return to Japan on those days.

What with one thing and another, we finally returned to Japan, safe and sound. I was immediately called in by Tokuma, and I was in for a surprise. Off the top of his head he recited a list of the various events and award ceremonies that had taken place while I was away. "Where were you on these days, when all these events were taking place?" He spouted the list from memory. "You planned it this way, didn't you?" he said. "I'm not blind, you know." He was really pissed off. "I knew what you were up to! And who do you think had to attend those events? Me, that's who!" Over the telephone he had been pleasant enough, without the slightest indication that he was displeased. But the whole time he had been planning how to call me on the carpet.

By this time I was pretty used to his ways and simply retorted, "To recite that long list without any notes! That's really impressive. You must have practiced ahead of time." And it *was* impressive, learning a list like that by heart. I had to give him that.

### The Last Years

The last three years or so before President Tokuma passed away, aside from times when I had a previous engagement, I was often summoned to meet with him in the evening. His secretary would call to make the arrangements.

It would be an invitation to have dinner together. Tokuma always had dinner at a restaurant called Yamazato in the Hotel Okura, where I would join him. Physically this wasn't as easy as it sounds. In the morning I would see him at the Tokuma Shoten offices and then go to Studio Ghibli in Koganei, returning to the Tokuma offices in Shinbashi in the evening when summoned by President Tokuma; finally, after dinner with him, I would end the day by returning to Ghibli. It was hard, but what Tokuma had to say was always interesting, and I learned a lot from him. It was an invaluable experience.

Incidentally, Tokuma was also popular with women. I didn't hear this directly from him; I got it secondhand from a certain woman. When she asked him what he did when he was being pursued by a fan, he gave this interesting answer: "In that case, I just fall down and play dead, and they pass on by." I'm not sure what he meant by "fall down," but somehow it seemed to make sense, and there was nothing for me to worry about.

# 7 For Making Things, Small Companies Are the Best

## Ghibli as a "Small Neighborhood Factory"

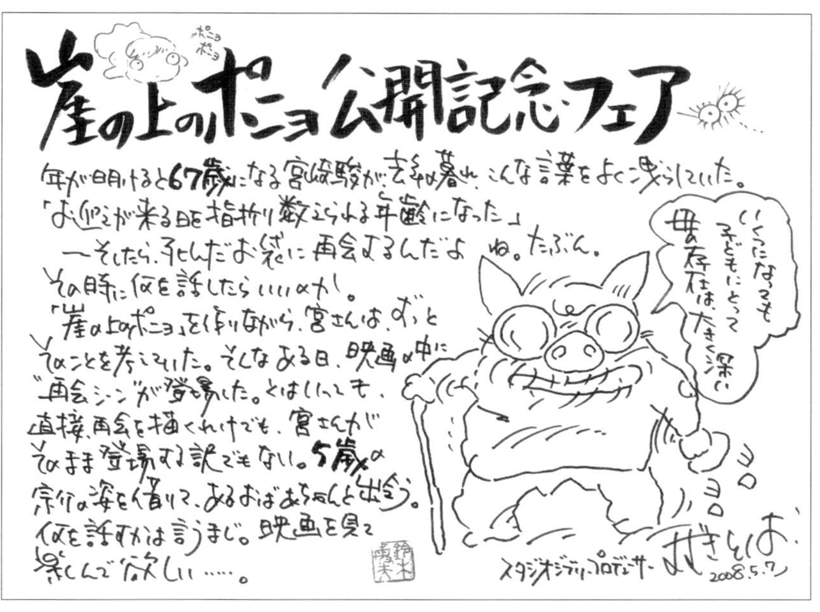


An advertising panel created by Toshio Suzuki in 2008 for display in bookstores to commemorate the release of *Ponyo on the Cliff by the Sea.* The sketch satirically captures the doddery appearance of Hayao Miyazaki at the age of sixty-seven. The handwritten text tells of how Miyazaki looks forward to being reunited with his now-deceased mother. This yearning is reflected in the movie in the scene where the five-year-old Sosuke meets with a certain old woman. For the words they exchange, the reader is advised to see the movie.

**Toshio Suzuki**

Exercising proper scheduling and budgeting, Ghibli's goal has been to devote itself wholeheartedly to each and every film it has undertaken, not to compromise in any way whatsoever. It has done this under the leadership of directors Miyazaki and Takahata, and by adhering to the tenet that the director is all-powerful. The fact that Ghibli has somehow been able to maintain this difficult stance for ten years, to realize both commercial success and proper business management, is due to the exceptional ability of these two directors and the efforts of the staff. This can be said to be the history of Studio Ghibli.

Frankly, I didn't think Ghibli would last as long as it has. When the company was initially established, the thinking was that if the first film was a success, we would try another; if the first failed, that would be the end of Ghibli. To reduce risk, at the beginning we didn't hire employees on a regular basis. For each new film a staff of about seventy people would be assembled, and when the film was done, they would be disbanded. This was the style we adopted....

To make something really good, that was Ghibli's goal. Maintaining the existence of the company and seeing it grow were secondary considerations. This is what sets Ghibli apart from the ordinary company.

("Sutajio Jiburi no junen" [Ten Years at Studio Ghibli]; 1995)

## Aspiring to be a Bystander

In hindsight, I have always considered myself a spectator to events. Even if I am one of the parties involved, I like to see myself as a bystander. In this sense, "bystander" usually has negative connotations, but I think the word has its merits. Bystanders are usually full of curiosity, and see things from a fairly objective point of view.

This reminds me of Seiichiro Ujiie of Nippon TV. Although he turned eighty-two this May (2008), he is still full of curiosity and has a strong desire to "capture the age." He started out as a journalist for the *Yomiuri* newspaper, so it is understandable that he should want to observe how things were developing in the world, both as a bystander and as a dedicated newsman. The fact that I get along very well with Ujiie is probably due to the similarity of our thinking in this regard. In that connection, I remember reading (or misreading) Yoshie Hotta's novel *Hiroba no kodoku* and thinking how right he was, that this is what the role of a third party should be.

I am sometimes asked whether I feel I am under pressure, and my answer is "very rarely." Even when the issue at hand is the future of Studio Ghibli, I somehow feel it's a matter that concerns someone else. I don't often take matters too seriously, but observe them rather objectively. This is quite an important quality, I think. I have my parents to thank for this gift.

It may sound paradoxical, but it is this quality that enables me to conduct thoroughgoing simulations when faced with a problem, and to consider carefully all possible alternatives. At such times as this, any feelings of either anxiety or overeagerness would just get in the way.

## Is This the End?

Studio Ghibli was established in 1985 following the success of *Nausicaä*. Many people may think that it was all smooth sailing after that, but they would be wrong. The reality was quite the opposite. People in the film industry, especially those concerned with distribution, were wondering when the end would come. They took the view that if the latest film achieved a certain percentage of what its predecessor had, that would be fine, but if it didn't, that would presage the coming of the end. The rubric of "If one succeeds, we'll try another; if it fails, that's the end" was not just rhetoric; it indicated an ever-present sense of imminent disaster.

This was powerfully brought home with a vengeance with the release of *Totoro* and *Grave of the Fireflies* as a double feature. One person connected with the film industry told me frankly, "I guess this is the end of Ghibli." This comment was understandable, since in comparison to *Nausicaä*'s 915,000 admission and *Castle in the Sky*'s 775,000, the double feature had only drawn 450,000 admissions (with a second release adding another 150,000). Ultimately it attained only half the numbers that *Nausicaä* had. This was apparently why people thought Ghibli was not long for this world.

This came to me as a shock. Did people really think in that way, I wondered. Up to this point, the only thing in my mind was to make something that was truly of high quality. All my thoughts had been devoted to that; I paid little attention to commercial success. But now, belatedly, I painfully realized that the goal was to make a film that viewers would come to see precisely because it was a good film, that would bring them to the theaters and produce a commercial success. It was at this juncture that I first began to seriously contemplate the issue of advertising.

## First and Foremost, the Title

In thinking about advertising, I realized that the title had a high priority. The title determines the direction of the film and at times is the film's best ad copy. This thinking reflects my experience as a magazine editor. Depending on the title for a feature issue, magazine sales can vary wildly.

Since the title determines the direction of the film, it has to be treated with extra care. It is the strongest message indicating the nature of the film, so it has to read well as ad copy. That has been my stance since *Nausicaä.*

> *In the case of* Kaze no tani no Naushika *[Nausicaä of the Valley of the Wind], there had been some disagreement about the title. The promotion producer then, Masaya Tokuyama, was against it, arguing that it wouldn't contribute to sales. He suggested* Kaze no senshi Naushika *[Nausicaä, Warrior of the Wind]. I put up a big fight. But it was not only Tokuyama who insisted on a change but also the distributor, Toei. It took quite a long time to bring them around. But just think about it. The title is closely tied to the heart of the film. To protect the title is to protect the film you are attempting to make. If you compromise, you are giving up on the film. We went on and on about this, seemingly without end....*
>
> *Of the titles that Miya-san thought up,* Kurenai no buta *[Porco Rosso] is the best of all. When I showed it to the copywriter, essayist, and actor Shigesato Itoi, he said, "There is no better copy than this." Titles are extremely important.*
>
> (*Eiga doraku* [Mixing Film and Pleasure]; 2005)

The next question was how to make the title more widely known. What surfaced here was the issue of external support. Nowadays such support is taken as a matter of course and appears almost invariably in the credits as *tokubetsu kyosan,* or "special support." In the case of Ghibli, however, things were different. While special support ordinarily indicates financial support toward production costs, at Ghibli it was limited to cooperative or joint advertising without financial input. This is what we now call a "tie-in." If the studio relied on outside help for production costs, there was bound to be a detrimental effect on the production process, which is exactly why special support was limited to advertising. At the time of *Castle in the Sky* and *Kiki's Delivery Service*, the older thinking was still partially in effect, and the new policy was a reflection of the experience garnered from those two films.

Even with this type of limited advertising support, however, the benefits were huge. In the business world it is commonly said that advertising for a new product costs 1 billion yen: 500 million for name recognition and another 500 million for information concerning the nature of the product. In our case, since we needed to have a good many people come and see our work, we had to advertise to make the title widely known. In that sense, it was no different from introducing a new product. But there was no way we could possibly come up with that amount of money. Thus the fact that other companies would undertake cooperative or joint advertising on our behalf was, to say the least, very welcome. For these companies, on the other hand, the fact that they were supporting Ghibli's films improved their image. This is what gave birth to the first cooperative efforts with Nippon TV and others, and later led us to approach additional firms to develop the optimum advertising campaign for each film.

### The Point of *Pom Poko*

I have already mentioned this title in chapter 5 as one that was subject to heated discussion. Since the title indicates the gist of a film, it is usually a lack of total confidence in it that leads to disagreement. In this case, there appeared to be not only indecision but a lack of commitment—the worst possible scenario. This caused me, as the producer, to send out a memo to everyone concerned with advertising—about twenty people in all, including Nippon TV and Toho.

> *Was it just a coincidence that the popular sports newspapers devoted little space to the press conference announcing* Pom Poko*?*
>
> *The answer is "No, it wasn't." At the press conference everyone*

*from the presidents of the investing companies on down were full of fatuous praise for burgeoning Ghibli, declaring arrogantly that "our goal should be film rentals of 3 billion yen, if not 5 billion." Even I, a former reporter, couldn't bring myself to endorse such nonsense. "It's on your head," is what I wanted to say. In the end, no one on the dais uttered the usual modest phrases, such as "We are creating something really interesting. In order for it to be seen by a wide audience, we need your help." It was as though everyone had been struck dumb.*

*The usual deluge of journalists that descends on Ghibli after a press conference was this time virtually nil. This, too, was not a coincidence. What materialized, instead, were requests to piggyback products on the film. Rather than supporting the movie, they wanted to take advantage of any popularity the film might have. . . .*

*I forgot to mention this earlier, so I will do it here to be on the safe side. The greatest attraction of Ghibli films is that they are always fresh and inventive. I have continually emphasized this point in the advertising. The present film,* Pom Poko, *is also full of fresh content. But for some reason this fact has not come across. Why should that be? Is it because there was not a clear direction? Or is it due to the pressure of "failure not being acceptable"?*

*Let's take a look at past films.* Kiki's Delivery Service *was about a girl in her teens.* Only Yesterday, *with a twenty-seven-year-old protagonist, was a film for adult women.* Porco Rosso *highlighted its difference from previous Miyazaki films and stressed that children needn't come to see it because it was mostly a love story between adults. Considered objectively, they were all taking a risk, but these risks turned out to be the key to their success.*

("Botamochi-san Manpuku-ji hondo hameita no itazura" [Graffiti on the Wooden Panels at the Main Hall of Botamochi-san Manpuku-ji]; 1994)

Then I continued in the memo with whatever I could think of to promote *Pom Poko* by emphasizing its prominent feature, its dumbfounding element. What we were most afraid of was being told that Ghibli had become predictable and boring. *Pom Poko* had the capacity to avert such criticism, and so it was decided to push this "toxic" capacity to the forefront. Ghibli was all about the challenge; that is what we wanted to say.

Looking back on it now, it is apparent how young I was. The script was written in one fell swoop, with very few revisions. At the end of the memo I quoted above, I borrowed some wording from a previous report in order to revisit the roots of this film.

> *Concerning* Pom Poko *and its advertising, the first thing that everybody noticed from the advertising copy was that raccoons appeared throughout, shifting themselves into various shapes. It was a fun-filled film with raccoons transmogrifying and transfiguring themselves, and goblins and shape-shifters playing a prominent role; it was the first work in Japanese filmography depicting a hilarious struggle between humans and raccoons. Some saw it as a condemnation of the destruction of nature by humankind. Others viewed it as a valiant struggle on the part of the adorable, endearing raccoons. Since it was a film with so many facets, all of these different views are valid in their own way, but depending on which you choose as the main advertising slogan, the overall view can change.*
>
> *While the film classifies itself as a* kassen *["war"] movie, it clearly does not depict the raccoons as transforming themselves into an army and fighting heroically with human beings on an equal footing, only to meet with a tragic end. As for the "transformations," they might cause viewers to grin broadly and laugh uproariously, but the transmogrification antics are not enough to make them shout "Bravo" with their eyes wide in wonder.*
>
> *The raccoons do their best, but it is mostly in vain. Their end can only be described as absurd and senseless. What a pity. The rac-*

*coons are engaged in a one-sided struggle, tilting at windmills. It is this that moves most viewers in the end.*

### Always Be Resolute

Just as I did with *Pom Poko*, having reconfirmed the importance of advertising in the 1990s and onward, I am now in the habit of writing an internal memo at each important juncture in a film's advertising campaign. One goal is to see that the entire staff is on the same page; another is to convince investors and the theatrical exhibitors of the film's value.

Theatrical exhibitors are generally pessimistic. Or, to give it a more positive slant, they are largely dubious. Compared with the preceding film, what kind of box office can the present film expect? That's what they are interested in. Whether for a Takahata film or a Miyazaki film, the same thinking applies. And *Pom Poko* was a movie about raccoons, wasn't it? Everyone in the industry was worried. I thought I had to put as positive a light on the matter as possible, and do it resolutely.

For this reason, whether in an internal memo or a verbal communication, I basically present my case very forcefully. Since I am one of the principal parties in the film's advertisement, I can't afford to be weak or wishy-washy. Otherwise, people will end up wondering what to think.

At heart I am a rather indecisive person, so I agonize over decisions before arriving at a conclusion. But once I get past the agonizing phase, I make up my mind and stick to it. I no longer waver. It is generally true that one can't hope for 100 percent certainty. Figuratively speaking, the most one can ask for is 90 or 80 percent certainty. In extreme cases, the certainty level may be only 51 percent. This happens when a certain choice appears to be better but one is not absolutely confident. But particularly in cases like this, one can't take the time to explain the process of comparing the choices; there comes a moment when one has to say which it is that one favors. Once a decision has been made, it should be presented with 100 percent confidence. This is the way a decision should be communicated. Of course, once you have taken a position, you need the ability to see it through.

Sometimes what you decide is unrealistic, or sometimes it needs refining. In such cases, you can only take the bit in your teeth and frankly admit it. That is good enough, I think. If you take a weak-kneed approach and say, "I am not really sure about this, but I tend to think…," staff won't know what they should do. Some might say that representing a 51 percent certainty as 100 percent is bound to be stressful, but it doesn't bother me.

### How to Conduct Meetings

After confirming the importance of advertising, I consciously began to conduct a series of meetings dealing with the subject. Particularly from the time of *Kiki's Delivery Service* and *Only Yesterday*, these meetings produced an unexpected number of new ideas and were a great deal of fun. Although huge in number, they all shared certain features. Let me list some of these features.

*Meetings Should be Fun.* If we are going to all the trouble of holding a meeting, it should at least be fun, and the participants should later be able to say that it was well worth attending. Otherwise, new ideas won't be forthcoming, and good films won't be born. Moreover, since meetings often last into the middle of the night, well outside of normal working hours, it would be a shame if the attendees didn't at least enjoy them.

*Ensure the Attendance of Younger Staff.* Attendees of such meetings consist of not only staff from Ghibli, but also people from concerned companies such as Nippon TV, Hakuhodo, and Dentsu. The fact that a variety of people participate has meaning in itself. When there is talk about "what happened at the office today," such small talk usually reflects the most up-to-date "modern" ideas. I always ask that young people be brought to the meetings. There is no need for them to be professionals in the field. The fact that they are young and inexperienced results in new ideas, which often prove quite useful. Among the attendees there are some people who you can expect to produce a certain opinion, and there are some who are completely unpredictable. What is needed is a mixture of professionals and amateurs, but it is the latter who are the most important. The most useless are those who pretend to know more than they do. Finding someone who is inexperienced but has good taste is the most gratifying, and I sometimes ask this individual's boss if I can borrow him or her. If I can find one or two people like that for a film, I have the feeling that I can count on them and that things will go well. With the new ideas they contribute, advertising can take an entirely new direction.

*Give Everyone a Chance to Speak.* No matter how trivial a matter might seem, I ask everyone their opinion. Of course, this takes time. I have spent four or five hours on a rough draft for a flyer. But this mostly has to do with fundamental matters. Once the fundamentals are understood, the rest is relatively easy. My magazine experience has proven useful here. At the time, aside from the editors, there were fifty or sixty writers. One at a time I asked them what we should take up next. It was my job to winnow out the best ideas, to listen and be taught. This work is somewhat similar to traffic control. Once an idea had been decided on, I make the person who came up with the idea responsible for carrying it out. This motivates that person and produces the best results.

*Don't Come to Meetings with Preconceived Opinions.* When conducting meetings I indicate the general direction of the discussion, the theme, but I don't come armed with a fixed opinion. As much as possible, I approach the meeting with an open mind. To my way of thinking, that promotes a freer exchange of opinion and gives rise to new ideas. It is my job to listen and learn.

In any event, in the end I have to consolidate the various views. When I have reached a conclusion, I try to persuade the others as to its validity. The discussion goes on for as long as it takes, everyone sharing the same time and space. Sometimes it takes until morning. But this is actually fun. Anyone who doesn't enjoy this type of thing will not have been invited to the meeting in the first place—just people who want to be there.

I might mention here that I don't keep a record of what has transpired. I don't take notes. What is important will remain in your mind, I believe. However, later on, if I hear an account of the meeting from someone who has kept objective notes, that too can be very instructive.

### Good Films Give Advertising Meaning

The first film which was the object of serious advertising was *Kiki's Delivery Service*. It attracted far more viewers than any of its predecessors and was a huge success. Thereafter *Only Yesterday*, *Porco Rosso*, and *Pom Poko* were also hits. In 1995, the tenth anniversary of Ghibli's founding, it was decided that I would give a lecture at the world-famous Annecy International Animated Film Festival, which takes place every June in the beautiful city of Annecy in southeastern France. I spoke about Ghibli advertising as quoted below.

I should mention here, however, that rather than "speaking" I was actually reading a Japanese speech that had been translated into English. For some inexplicable reason Takahata was in the audience, listening to my presentation. That made me feel very uneasy. He told me later, "Your pronunciation wasn't bad. But when you said '*Nausicaä of the Valley of the Wind*,' 'wind' sounded like 'window.'" That's Takahata for you, always saying more than is needed. [Laughs] Here I will quote a bit from that speech.

> *What makes Studio Ghibli unique is that it has achieved recognition for not only its renowned quality but also its huge success at the box office. It seems that no matter how hard filmmakers work and*

*how great films being made are, in a country like Japan where film-making is neither particularly encouraged nor nurtured, closure due to financial difficulties is just a matter of time.*

*Recently, Ghibli's films have been performing reliably well at the box office. There are mainly three reasons for this.*

*The first is obviously the high quality.... Without this emphasis on quality workmanship, continued success cannot be attained, no matter how great the marketing effort.*

*The second reason has to do with the accumulation of Ghibli.... As each new film was released, it was nurtured by the success of the previous films, creating a kind of lucky chain.*

*The third reason is a definite marketing policy.... Nowadays, a film cannot attract a large audience just because it is a good film. It must become a kind of event, made so by a vast marketing plan. For example, Ghibli films are usually released in the summer. Therefore, the mandate is to create a nationwide atmosphere that "everyone is saying this movie is the must-see film of the summer...."*

*When animation is mentioned in Japan, there is always the inevitable impression that it is something for children. However, the fact is that a film cannot become a hit if it doesn't attract a female audience, and it is also extremely important to win the favor of parents and their children. That is precisely why, with Ghibli films, we conduct advertising that is full range, aiming at viewers from children to adults. It is especially important to present the film as being of a quality that will satisfy discerning adult eyes.*

Perhaps because I was speaking before a foreign audience, my talk was unusually well organized. Ironically, this might give the wrong impression, I thought, which is why I prefaced my remarks by saying that it might seem that I was patting ourselves on the back and implying that everything went according to plan, but the reality was somewhat different. To a large extent, I said, the flow of events produced these fortunate results. They should keep that in mind. What I wanted to convey is that the high quality of the films is of ultimate importance. That has been true from the very beginning, and it is, more than anything else, what gives advertising its meaning.

### *Princess Mononoke* as a Turning Point.

As I said in my speech at Annecy, although Ghibli films have steadily produced good box office returns, theatrical exhibitors still didn't always have high expectations. What finally produced the formula "Ghibli equals expectation" was the blockbusting success of *Princess Mononoke* (1997). In hindsight it may seem ironical, but the film most shrouded by negativity was actually *Mononoke*.

This was related to the fact that production costs had grown astronomically. As it happened, immediately after Annecy, when *Mimi o sumaseba* (Whisper of the Heart; 1995) was showing signs of success, I discussed with Miya-san what our next step should be, and the result was that the first film in Ghibli's new phase should be *Princess Mononoke*.

> *Thankfully,* Whisper of the Heart *was a big hit. But this didn't prevent us from worrying. What concerned us was the question of whether or not we should just plunge ahead into the next film.... After a good deal of thought, we came up with the following:*
>
> *1. There should be a one-year gap between film release dates.*
>
> *2. Each work should take two years to complete, and should result in a film that is rich in content and contains something intriguing that has never before been seen, showcasing Ghibli's reappearance after a year's hiatus. It was this or nothing, we thought.*
>
> *Until then, Ghibli had taken one working year to produce a film.... About 80 percent of the production costs of an animation are consumed by wages. If the period of time devoted to production was*

Illustrations by Toshio Suzuki of three protagonists in Miyazaki films: Porco (*Porco Rosso*), Clarisse (*The Castle of Cagliostro*), and San (*Princess Mononoke*). By drawing principal figures and scenes with his own hand, Suzuki attempted to grasp an overall feel for each film.

> *doubled, production costs would automatically double. We realized that.*
>
> *But in terms of content, technique, and staff, Ghibli had always been at the leading edge, and these factors were necessary and sufficient conditions for Ghibli to forge its way into the future.*
>
> ("Eiga 'Mononoke-hime' setsumei shiryo" [Explanatory Material for the Film *Princess Mononoke*]; 1996)

To double the production time and increase the interval between releases to one year meant taking a huge business risk.

The production costs of *Mononoke* were predicted to be four times that of *Porco Rosso* and two and a half times those of *Pom Poko*. The difference was obvious to one and all. Almost all associated parties were against this approach, and it was not easy to convince them otherwise. The explanatory material for the film started with a straightforward view of its significance and then went on to a discussion of when costs could be recouped. My thinking was that since it was a film, its break-even point should be achieved by theatrical box office earnings alone, but since there was a need to convince banks of the film's viability, I also included TV licensing fees and DVD revenue, providing a fairly detailed list.

In spite of my efforts at persuasion, however, resistance to the film remained deep-rooted. There was even a conspiratorial movement among our collaborators to force us to abandon the project. In this case, I resorted to drastic measures. I called in the ringleader of the clique, told him he was no longer welcome at Ghibli, and broke off all relations. This kind of thing is sometimes necessary. Nevertheless, *Mononoke* not only surpassed its projected 4 million admissions (its immediate predecessor, *Pom Poko,* had drawn 3.25 million) but reached the unheard-of figure of 14.2 million.

*Spirited Away* was the first film for which the theatrical exhibitors held any expectations. Of course, the "expectation" was that it should do at least as half as well as *Princess Mononoke*. In fact, however, it broke the previous record and garnered an unheard-of 24 million admissions. When the release date of the next film, *Howl's Moving Castle*, was scheduled, other films, including live-action movies and foreign films, were withdrawn from the release list for fear of a schedule conflict with *Howl*. Previously, everyone had been wondering when Ghibli would flop, but now expectations were absurdly high. That in itself became cause for concern. It was a little scary to have everyone expecting success; it was much easier on the mind to have them unsure of themselves.

## Advertising That Doesn't Advertise

At a recent gathering I was talking with Seiichiro Ujiie of Nippon TV. At one point he said, "I envy you. If you advertise a movie, you always get a hit." I couldn't help but raise my voice a bit and reply, "If that were the case, how easy life would be!" He sat there for a moment, thinking about it. He's the type of person who always takes what people say seriously.

Essentially, the way advertising is conducted differs from film to film. You must have a feeling for the times or things will not go well. And simple mass advertising does not guarantee success. When things do go well, what makes you happiest of all is the fact that you have correctly judged the mood of the day.

Take *Howl's Moving Castle*, for example. Our principal advertising strategy was that we wouldn't advertise. Ordinarily, advertising presents the essence of the product. This time, though, rather than trying to do that, we were going to limit the amount of information offered. I figured that this in itself would be a kind of entertainment. "Howl is coming" would be our only message. I wrote the following for the press material when the film was launched.

> *Advertising is indispensable to any film, but this time there wouldn't be any. No, to put it more precisely, there wouldn't be any detailed*

> *commentary on the nature of the film or its theme. We wanted viewers to see the film with an open mind, without any preconceptions. This was Hayao Miyazaki's ardent desire.*
>
> *This approach was the result of my reflecting on the advertising for* Spirited Away, *which had been viewed as excessive. But then, the moment I made up my mind to try this approach there were protests from certain quarters who usually supported Ghibli. We want to help you, they seemed to be saying, but not if you are going to ignore our well-intentioned efforts. As much as possible I met with these individuals one at a time and earnestly presented my case.*
>
> *What is the right amount of advertising? During this period we discussed this issue any number of times, including with the general staff. Rather than talking about the content of the advertising, we spent a lot of time talking about amount. Quality is more important than quantity, isn't it? Advertising is just a means of attracting attention, isn't it? When commonsensical views like this were presented, the whole staff breathed a sigh of relief.*
>
> ("Senden shinai 'senden'" ["Advertising" that Doesn't Advertise; 2004])

What had triggered this ruckus was Miya-san's "ardent desire." When *Spirited Away* turned out to be a hit, a lot of people had told him, "The film was good, and the advertising was fabulous." This really bothered him. He went around asking staff, "Was the movie a hit because of the advertising? What do you think?"

While it is true that it was Miya-san's "desire" that had set the new advertising in motion, I also had my own perspective. I had noticed that the success of the films released that summer didn't necessarily reflect the size of their advertising budgets. I was just pondering what could be done about this when it occurred to me that producing no marketing material at all might have some meaning. When marketing material is available, mass media tends to follow its lead. But this time, without such material, mass media reporters would actually have to view the film and write what they felt. The result would be reviews with fresh insight, and that would have the same effect as advertising. This is what I thought, in any case.

## Believing in the Power of Words

Thinking further about the matter, I came to realize that the job of a producer lies in his use of words. He should communicate what is needed to the many people involved in the making of a film and create a message directed at those who would potentially watch the film. It all depends on words. One of my aspirations has been "to make the incomprehensible comprehensible." The medium for doing this is words.

Perhaps as a reflection of this, Mamoru Oshii, director of *Urusei yatsura* (Urusei Yatsura; a.k.a. Lam, the Invader Girl) and *Kido keisatsu patoreiba* (Mobile Police Patlabor), had this to say: "Since Miyazaki met up with Suzuki, his work has gotten boring." He seemed to be saying that since I had become involved with Miyazaki's films, a certain social element had been introduced, and this is what grated on his nerves. Oshii made the following comments in a dialogue published in the *Yomiuri* newspaper.

> *Oshii: Around the time* Nausicaä *was released, anime seemed to be shouldering the fate of the Earth and humankind. Even in TV animation series about school life, when they were made into a film, they suddenly became all about the Earth, all about Humankind. I was working on* Urusei yatsura *at the time, and I got tired of hearing "the Earth," "Humankind."*
>
> *Oshii: It all seemed so false to me. Their "holier than thou" attitude, their way of expressing things and their way of thinking, it rubbed me the wrong way.*
>
> *Oshii: [about Suzuki] The work of filmmakers is in some respects unconscious. They convert that unconscious aspect into words, which is*

> *good. But there is also a dangerous side to this. By explaining the film in words, its significance becomes fixed and incontrovertible.*
> (*Shinshun anime taidan: Suzuki Toshio vs. Oshii Mamoru* [New Year's Anime Dialogue: Toshio Suzuki vs. Mamoru Oshii], 2004)

This was Oshii's opinion, about which I could only think, "Is that really the case?" It was true that Miya-san's films hadn't included a social aspect until then. But this new aspect of Miya-san's work captured the hearts of the films' viewers, didn't it? In hindsight I can't help thinking that this is also true.

In any case, my goal is to "capture the present in words." My thinking in this respect is carried out via the words naturally accumulated in my many conversations with others. I don't take notes. They are words I have picked up along the way. When I write, they come rushing to the surface.

### Lies Have Their Uses

Whenever I think that a lie is not untrue from a broader perspective, I sometimes lie, or I don't mention what I know to be true. Following the Japanese adage that "lies are sometimes expedient," I don't let the fact that I have lied haunt me. That is, I am able to convince myself that the lie is not a lie.

There is, however, one lie that still bothers me. When the idea for making the manga *Nausicaä* into a film surfaced, I was asked by Hakuhodo how many copies of the book had been printed. In actuality, it had sold some 50,000 copies, but I quickly temporized and said 500,000. The thought had flashed across my mind that Hakuhodo might be reluctant to make the film if they were informed of the real figures. So I baldly misrepresented the truth, an out-and-out lie, of the type that lingers in the mind.

Here is another incident, one that has a touch of humor. Miya-san and I were to go to the U.S. on an advertising campaign for *Spirited Away*. There had been seventy requests for interviews from TV and the print media. I had trimmed the list a bit, but the number was still substantial. I knew for sure that Miya-san would think it too much trouble, so I told a little lie. I said, "There were a hundred requests for interviews, but I negotiated and reduced it to forty-five." Miya-san was as pleased as Punch with this and did all the interviews.

The next incident was not so much lying as feigning ignorance and failing to report the facts. This took place during the production of *Whisper of the Heart*. The basic concept had come from Miya-san, but the movie was actually directed by Yoshifumi Kondo. As completion of the film drew near and the sound was being mixed, I noticed that the transition between two scenes was a bit strange.

"Kondo-san, isn't this transition a bit odd?" I said.

"Well," he replied, "Miyazaki-san said it was alright."

"But no matter how you look at it, it's odd, I think," I said.

"Well, actually, I think so, too," he said, surprisingly.

"Okay, let's change it then," I told him, but he remained unconvinced, concerned about Miya-san's reaction.

"Let's go ahead and do it, and I'll take responsibility," I told him. "We can show it to Miya-san at the staff screening." This proved persuasive, and we changed the order of the scenes. But Kondo-san continued to worry about whether we should inform Miya-san ahead of time. I told him, "Don't worry about it. If we tell Miya-san now, you'll only be adding to his other worries. If you and I think it's okay, that should be enough."

When the day came for the staff screening, Kondo-san was on pins and needles, but after we had finished viewing the film, Miya-san didn't say a word about the problematic transition. He simply said, "Well done. Very well done."

In this case I think Miya-san was mistaken in the original transition. But in making a change there was no need for us to explain each little detail; if we took care of the problem, that should be enough. That was my thinking. After all, Miya-san is not a god. He sometimes makes mistakes. With that in mind, it's better for him, I tend to think, if we independently take care of some problems without informing him of every little detail.

## Can You Draw a Map?

One of a producer's most important tasks is to draw a rough sketch of the project. This means depicting the big picture and the general progress by means of a graph. In a sense it is equivalent to drawing a map, a sketch of the project in terms of time and space.

In that regard, last year (2007) I had a very interesting experience. As part of the NHK program *Kagai jugyo: Yokoso senpai* (Extracurricular Lessons: Welcome Alumni) I visited my childhood elementary school to give the students a special lesson. I decided to have them draw two maps. One would be an ordinary map, and the other would be the map of the locale in *Kiki's Delivery Service.*

I had told them ahead of time that the lesson would consist of drawing a map. Much to my surprise, they brought with them real maps or maps printed out on their computers. That just wouldn't do, so I had them put those away and draw maps of their own creation. The upshot was that hardly anyone could produce a map worthy of the name.

Again, surprisingly, when I told them, "Draw a map of your favorite place," each and every one of them said, "I don't have a favorite place." The end result was generally a nearby convenience store or supermarket, or at most a public park. They didn't drop by places on their way to or from school. They couldn't recall what kind of buildings there were. They weren't interested, so of course they didn't remember.

Their sense of distance was also funny. Their maps wouldn't fit on the paper, and ended only half-done or ran off the edge. When I talked with the students one at a time, it became evident that they had never

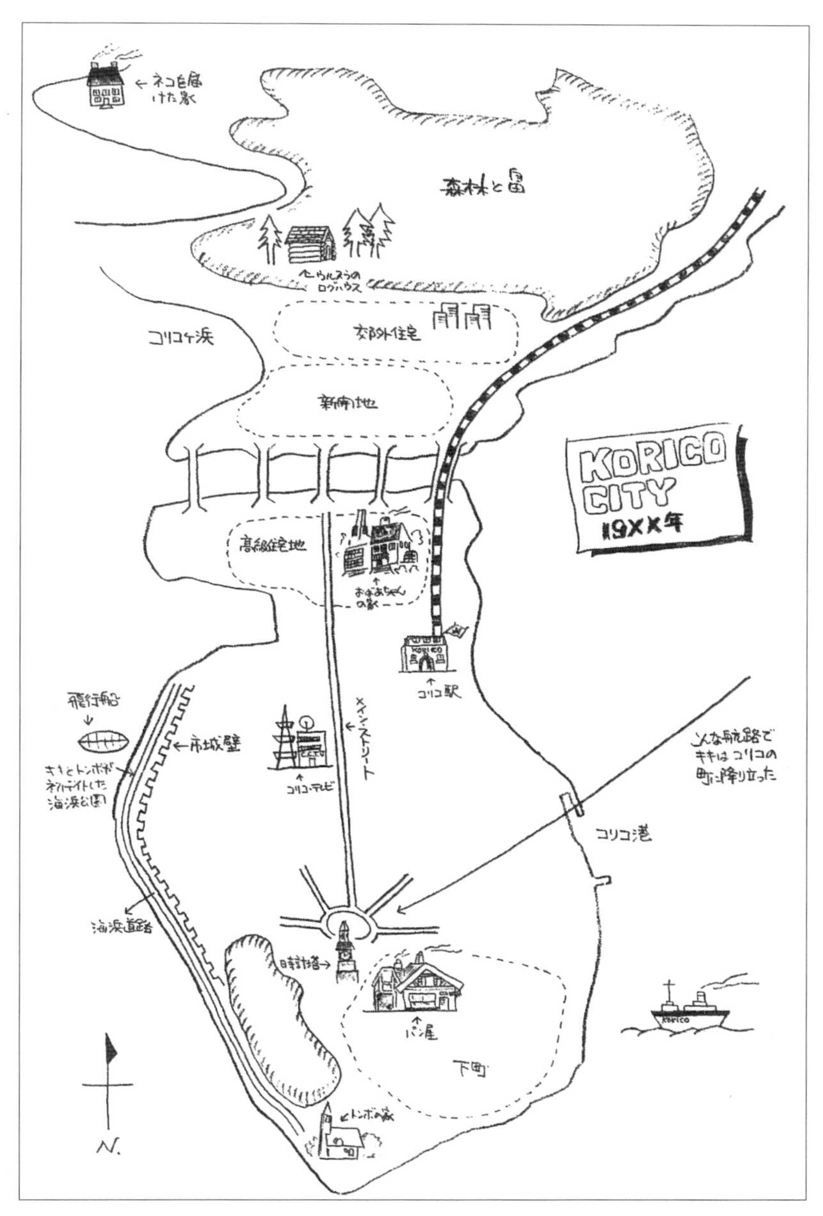


A map by Toshio Suzuki of the city that was the setting for *Kiki's Delivery Service*. It is one of the important jobs of a producer to create maps, whether based on real or imaginary worlds.

drawn a map until they reached the sixth grade. There was one student who did a good job, but this was the exception that proved the rule.

The next day, I had them create a map of the locale in an animated film, and the results were completely different. First I showed them *Kiki's Delivery Service*, which they all watched with immense interest. Next came the map. They worked away with intense concentration, and all the maps were well done. I pointed to two girls in the class and told them to put their maps up on the blackboard. When I asked, "Does anyone have any places they would like to fix?" a number of hands flew up. I chose several and had them make as many changes as they wanted. The resultant map was not much different from the one I had drawn; it was nearly perfect.

This left me with mixed feelings. The fact that these kids couldn't draw a real map meant that the surroundings they lived in held no sense of reality for them. But they were happy to draw a map of a movie locale, and it was accurate. They could even remember the dialogue. They were in a state of mind where the movie was closer to them than real life. Since I and other filmmakers had contributed to this phenomenon, I wasn't sure how I should feel about it.

In any case, I think that being able to draw a map is one of the basic skills one has to learn in life. For producers and editors, of course, the creation of rough sketches is part of their job, so they need to master it. Once you have the big picture in mind, the details later fall in place.

### Preserving the Original Rationale

Studio Ghibli was originally established to produce the films of Isao Takahata and Hayao Miyazaki. We created a company to do what they wanted to do. As the company achieved success, new possibilities came to the fore, and once it started to make headway as a business, the problem of management inevitably surfaced. What was our thinking about Ghibli as a business?

My answer was simple. "With the goal of producing good films, we should make use of the company as long as we can." It all came down to that. I was willing to devote myself wholly toward that end, but I was not at all interested in making the company larger. "To make good films and get a bit in return over the long run, that is happiness." So I thought at the time and still think today. The ideal was a small but quick-footed company. On this subject I once expressed my thoughts as follows:

> *In the world of animation, the only country that Disney is unable to dominate in terms of box office revenue is Japan. From Disney's perspective, it should be grossing two or three times what it does in the Japanese market, but for some reason this just doesn't happen. This situation gave rise to the idea of Disney tying up with Ghibli, renowned for* Princess Mononoke *and* Spirited Away, *and producing a film together. In fact, one offer after another has come in from Disney and DreamWorks. But for the moment we have no intention of working with them. Why? Because the differences in lifestyles, customs, and traditions between the two countries are too great, and the system of producing a film is too dissimilar. And it goes without saying that in order to create something really good, small companies are better than big ones.*
>
> *We took a tour of the Walt Disney Studios, which weren't so much studios as huge factories. In terms of technical staff alone, at one point I heard that they housed over a thousand people....*
>
> *However, even though there was a difference in scale, the process of producing an animated film was not all that dissimilar. What was radically different was the preparatory stage leading up to final planning.*
>
> ("'Sen to Chihiro' wa Dizuni ni katta" ["Spirited Away" Beats Disney]; 2002)

As a matter of fact, one aspect of company management is that it is hard to maintain a company without making it larger. On top of that, since the parent company (Tokuma Shoten) was burdened by debt, there was always a pressing demand for constant hits. But, on the other hand, if business logic were to rule the day, the company's reason for existence would get turned on its head; if this were the case, Ghibli would lose its original appeal. I often go so far as to say, "If Ghibli is no longer capable of producing good films, it is no longer needed." If you are not ready to go to that extent, I think, you can't preserve the company's original reason for being.

Ghibli's reason for being can be encapsulated in the word "challenge." Making safe, mundane films one after another is not challenging. What we want to do is create something entirely different from what we have done before. This thinking is reflected in the fact that, from *Mononoke* onward, we decided to make only one film every two years. This year, 2008, Takahata turns seventy-three and Miya-san sixty-seven. I myself will be sixty. But in our heart of hearts we haven't changed a bit since the early days.

Maybe this is the reason that the head of public relations, Jun'ichi Nishioka, goes around saying, "Day in and day out, you never know what will happen at this company. That's what makes it interesting." And in fact something usually happens. That, as he says, is what makes it interesting. To be able to continue on like this would be true happiness, I think.

### A Company That Makes Films

There is one more thing I shouldn't forget to say, which is that Ghibli is a company that makes films. You may think this hardly needs saying, but actually the matter is not all that simple.

In the old days, movies were made to be seen in movie theaters. That was the beginning and end of the story. But now the situation has changed, what with DVDs, TV, and character goods. Due to various circumstances, Ghibli has come to play a part in this world. The problem is that if this tendency escalates, it may eventually be forgotten that Ghibli was originally a filmmaker. In fact, I myself know of a number of production companies that have lost their way and their true roots.

Frequently, a film is referred to as *kontentsu* ("content"), a word that I particularly dislike. For the life of me, I can't see why a foreign word has to be used in this case. You may think I am being sophomorically pedantic, but what is being referred to is a "work" of cinematic art. Otherwise, films are put on the same level as DVDs, telecasts, and character goods. There is a certain order to things, I believe. If a film is a hit, then the others follow in due course. A film made with these secondary products solely in mind cannot be called a work of art.

Take, for example, the short films on view at the Ghibli Museum. At the moment there are six of them, but you can only see them by coming to the museum. Ordinarily they would be available on DVDs and sold at the museum shop, but that is not done either. In the past movies could only be seen by going to a theater; we have attempted to recreate that experience in a very small way. Nowadays you can easily get almost anything you desire. We wanted to create a kind of antithesis to that fact.

## Be a Professional Wherever You Go

Every year I tell newly hired employees the same thing. "We don't want people who will be satisfied by simply joining Ghibli. First and foremost, you should become a professional." We want you, I tell them, to develop the skills—say, as an animator—that will be of use wherever you go in the future. We want you to work as an individual, not as a cog in a wheel. Unless you think of yourself as striving to become a professional, not a pawn in an organization, working here is not easy. As someone who is fond of saying, "When the company is no longer useful, just get rid of it," I don't want to be responsible for the employees' lives and livelihoods. Of course, this may just be a way of evading responsibility. [Laughs]

Once, as proposed by Miya-san, Ghibli shut down for six months. This came about in the following way, as I wrote at the time.

> *Starting on August 1 Ghibli will cease operations for six months. Work on Director Miyazaki's new film will begin next year on February 1, but until then staff will be released from their duties. Until now, whenever there was a break in the schedule, we subcontracted work for TV, but this time we want you to do as you please for six months. However, on February 1 you should return to work full of vim and vigor. This will be considered a temporary layoff, and wages will be paid at two-thirds of the usual rate.*
>
> *I often tell young people that working for Ghibli is not what's important; what's important is becoming a valuable animator wherever they work. I even go so far as to say that if they happen to find rewarding work elsewhere during the break, there is no need to return to Ghibli. This causes some people to worry about the loss of valuable personnel, but as long as Ghibli continues to make intriguing films, employees will come back, I think. It's a gamble.*
>
> ("'Sen to Chihiro' wa Dizuni ni katta" ["Spirited Away" Beats Disney]; 2002)

As a matter of fact, there are good many animators who have left Ghibli and are actively working elsewhere. Talented people want to try working on the outside. They want to test their strength.

Of course, there are times when you would like a person to stay; you regret their leaving. But when someone expresses a wish to leave, basically I approve it. I send them off with my best wishes for their success.

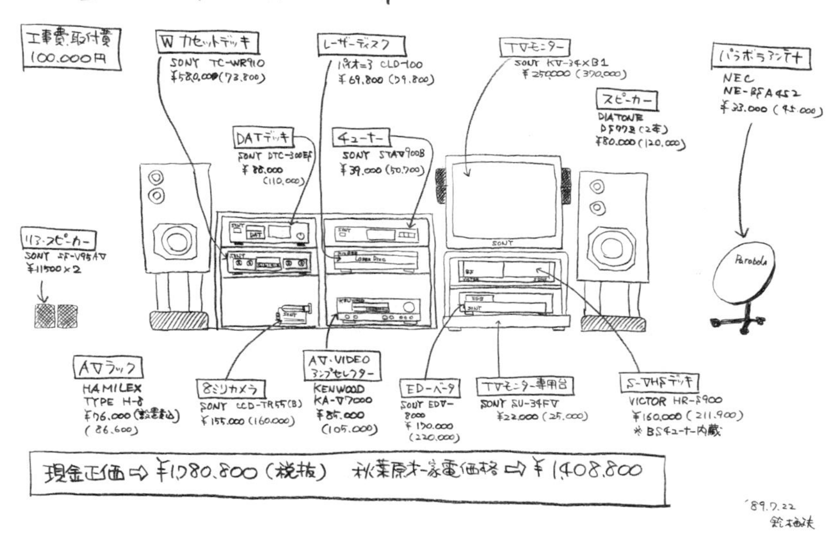


When Miyazaki built a mountain cabin in Shinshu, he told Suzuki, "I leave everything in your hands." This sketch shows Suzuki's plan for an AV setup. The work of realizing a director's ideas takes many forms.

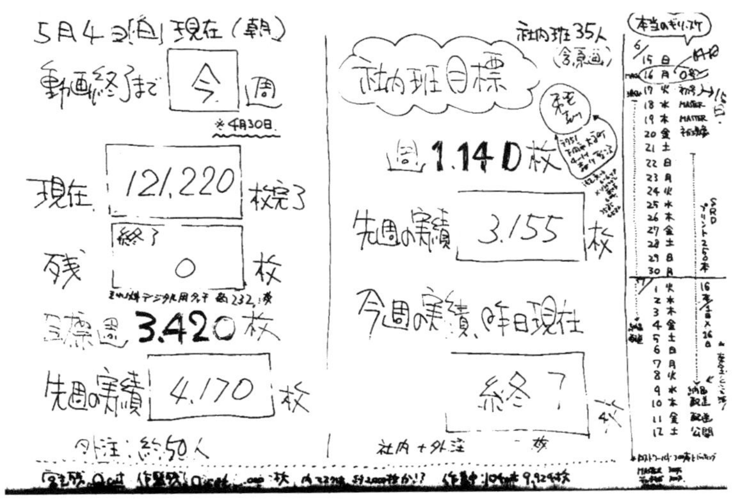


Production schedule for *Princess Mononoke*. Since the schedule was very tight, Suzuki would write it on a whiteboard, changing the numbers for the in-between drawings every day, and show the results to Miyazaki.

## A Craftsman Through and Through

Here is another telling incident. It involves a person I will call "A." He had been at Ghibli for more than ten years and was an animator of the first rank, employable by any studio. One day, out of the blue, he came to me and said he wanted to quit. "I have learned a lot at Ghibli," he said, "but I have also lost a lot. If I stay any longer, I don't think I can achieve my full potential. I want to try working somewhere else."

When I questioned him further, it turned out that his immediate reason for his wanting to leave was due to his devotion to his craft. In effect he said, "I intentionally drew something rather poorly, but Miyazaki-san didn't catch it. His judgment must be failing. There is no longer any reason for me to stay here."

But we didn't part on bad terms, and I sometimes asked for his help. I particularly remember an exchange that took place during the making of *My Neighbors the Yamadas*. Though it may not be obvious to everyone, *The Yamadas* has accomplished something that is very difficult for an animated film. If you look at the serialized manga, you will see that the heads of the characters are extraordinary large. Animating these characters is not easy. Due to the shortness of the legs, movement inevitably becomes unnatural. The individual in charge of *The Yamadas* at Ghibli was another highly capable animator, whom I will call "B." He was working on the scene where the tipsy father walks into a room and sits down at a low table. The problem was how to get him to sit down with such short legs. Done by an inept animator, the drawing was bound to look unnatural. Even at Ghibli there were only a handful of animators who could do the job properly. "B" was one of these few people, but since "A" was also extraordinarily talented, "B" asked for his help. "A" tried to put him off, but since he was interested in the problem, he asked "B" how he was going to get the character to walk. "B" held up two fingers and moved them like two legs walking. "Something like this," he said. "A" commented, "Yes,

I can see that." It was very interesting, like listening to two martial artists discussing tactics. This is the kind of exchange that is only possible between two master craftsmen.

After spending time here and there, "A" is now working at Ghibli again. Though he is perfectly qualified, there wasn't another place where he could put his ability to use. I asked him if he wouldn't like to become a Ghibli employee once again. He replied, "After leaving the company of my own volition, I don't think it's good to suddenly show up and say I'm a Ghibli employee again."

Well, what happened after that? The fact is that Ghibli has four studios. The fourth is situated at some distance from the others, in a rented house on the other side of the station. At my suggestion this studio was set up for individuals who are very good but who can't keep to a schedule. They can't arrive on time in the morning and leave on time in the evening. This studio was made for them. That's where we have "A" work. At present he is contributing enormously to *Ponyo*.

This fourth studio was set up as a means of attracting talented animators. Once every two years we recruit new employees and educate them in-house, but that alone is not enough. How we can attract new blood from the outside—people who are already developed animators—is always on my mind. All of the good animators are getting along in years, you see.

In passing I might say that Miya-san still does his own drawing, but what preys on his mind is the question of whether there is someone on the staff who is better than he is. One reason he is still active in this regard is that he only does work that he is confident of doing. This is a kind of paradox. The fact that his work is still up to standard is a source of personal pride on the one hand, but the fact that there is no one who surpasses him yet is a source of worry. This can be seen in the workplace even today.

## Function Alone Does Not Make an Organization

Filmmaking requires individuals of extraordinary talent, of course, but it also requires people who are steadily faithful to their appointed tasks. As a matter of fact, it is impossible for a film to be made by talented individuals acting alone; a film is the product of a number of people coming together and implementing the ideas of one individual. Both parties are needed—the talented ones with the ideas and the other individuals who put these ideas faithfully into effect.

The office atmosphere is created by the majority of honest, faithful individuals. The talented individuals who occasionally appear on the scene will sometimes leave the company and sometimes return, according to circumstances. Miya-san and I think there is nothing wrong with this.

As a model for this way of thinking, I found Jules Verne's *Deux Ans de Vacances* (Two Years' Vacation) particularly interesting. I once wrote the following about this novel.

> *Among the boys appearing in* Deux Ans de Vacances, *there is not one who is perfect, which is why all fifteen have to combine their individual strengths. This is what is interesting about the story. In managing an organization, this kind of collaboration is also the ideal. Each individual has something not possessed by the others; there are no dropouts, no restructuring. I ask myself: Isn't it possible to create this type of organization in real life? In fact, in my secret heart, I would one day like to make a film based on* Deux Ans de Vacances. ("Eigazukuri mo ryutsu mo, jidai no kawarime ni bokura wa iru" [In Filmmaking and Distribution, We Reside at a Turn of the Times]; 2005)

In contrast to this way of thinking stands the Shinsengumi, a group of swordsmen organized to protect the shogunate in the late 19th century. It was probably the first and last organization in Japan whose members were chosen by function alone. They were all swordsmen whose specialty was cutting down people with a sword. The Shinsengumi viewed people as function, and tried to form an organization based on function alone. As we all know, the Shinsengumi met a tragic end.

The question of the extraordinarily talented vis-à-vis average people, the balance between ability and faithfulness, this is a difficult issue, but there is no doubt in my mind that both are needed. If there is someone who is serious in his work but technically lacking, others can help him out. Sometimes it happens that in trying to lend a helping hand, the helper himself discovers something new and benefits as a result. That is the good side of working as a group. With an assemblage of lone wolves, the strength of the organization is only a matter of addition, though it can sometimes be unlucky subtraction. In actual fact, the Shinsengumi fought among themselves. In a situation where you are helping and being helped by others, the result is equivalent to multiplication.

It is not a matter of there being one superstar and the rest doing as they are told. I may be an idealist, but I much prefer everyone working together in collaboration. Every day is so much more fun.

## Someone Who Relieves the Stress

To say a bit more about this subject, I think that the atmosphere of an office benefits from the presence of a personality who relieves general stress. I have a good person to illustrate this point. He is Naoya Fujimaki of Hakuhodo DY Media Partners, who sang the theme song for *Ponyo*. When in college he sang in the group Marichanzu (Marichans), took a two-year leave of absence from school, and entered Hakuhodo, and before long he had become an important figure there. Just recently he formed the band Fujioka Fujimaki with Takaaki Fujioka from his university group and has started performing again. He reminds me of the TV dramas of the screenwriter and novelist Taichi Yamada, of which I am very fond. They always feature an utterly hopeless character who nevertheless possesses a certain engaging charm. Fujimaki-san is exactly this type of person.

He is not the kind of person who is always busily at work—far from it. He was in charge of Ghibli at Hakuhodo when *Neko no ongaeshi* (The Cat Returns, 2002) was being made, but he did virtually nothing. There were no tie-ins with other companies. At Hakuhodo he would leave a message saying that he would be at Ghibli, and phone calls for him would come every day, but in fact he never showed up. Since our goal was to make a success of *The Cat Returns*, I called him in. "I'm sorry," he said, "but I'm doing my best." My response to this was, "No, I don't think you're doing anything at all."

The person in charge of Ghibli at Dentsu was Ryoichi Fukuyama, and he was producing results, but Fujimaki nothing. Given that, it seemed I had no choice. I told him, "We can leave the financing of the film to Hakuhodo, but for the tie-ins we will have to go with Dentsu." Ordinarily this should have left Fujimaki absolutely shame-faced. After all, Dentsu and Hakuhodo were rival advertising agencies, and Fukuyama was younger than Fujimaki. But Fujimaki only said, "Okay, I'll leave it up to Fuku-chan." [Laughs] Even more amazing was what happened after he returned to his office and reported to his department head. Naturally he got a dressing-down. "It's because you're so addlebrained! That's why things like this happen." In the midst of this, Fujimaki quietly said, "What are you going say to the managing director?" Realizing that now it would be his turn to be scolded, Fujimaki's boss suddenly returned to himself. "What should I do?" he said. Fujimaki then offered, "Should I go with you?" [Laughs] That's the kind of person Fujimaki is.

Miya-san and I both like people like this. There was also the time when my assistant Nobuko Shiraki came to me one day and said, "If you have a moment, there is something I would like to discuss." Saying that maybe it wasn't her place to comment on this, she went on: "I wonder why you are so friendly with Fujimaki-san. I really don't see how he can be of much use to you." This eventually reached Miya-san's ears, and he immediately called in Shiraki-san and explained to her why Fujimaki was important.

Even the other day, Fujimaki came to the office, and although Miya-san was terribly busy, he spent two hours talking with him. At one point he told him, "Fujimaki-san, you are totally ignorant about the world. I don't even think you are interested in it." I think that talking with Fujimaki provided Miya-san some relief from everyday stress.

### Thinking about the Younger Generation

Ghibli now consists of a good number of people who are the children of the baby-boom generation, the junior baby boomers. Although I hadn't previously felt much difference between the generations, I have now come to feel that each generation does have its own instinctive way of looking at things, making each slightly different.

Goro Miyazaki, the director of *Gedo senki* (Tales from Earthsea, 2006), is now about forty years old. According to him, "You shouldn't ask a junior baby boomer to do two things at the same time." He says if you ask them to do one thing, they will do it to the best of their ability, but if you ask them to do two, they will get confused. For people like me, having two projects provides a break; if things get tough with one, you can always escape to the other with an easy mind. Having just one would create extra pressure for me. Here there seems to be a definite difference in feeling. The most outstanding difference, though, is that junior baby boomers lack the "I may fail, but I'll give it my best shot" mentality. They can foresee what the results will be, and they don't want to try if it is going to end in failure. This is a problem, I think, because there are some things you can't know until you try them.

Another thing that has been bothering me recently is how the word "responsibility" is used. When something has gone wrong, there are a surprising number of juniors who will facilely say, "Sorry. I'm responsible for that." You could say they are being honest and forthright, but I can't bring myself to praise them. When, after careful consideration, it is not clear who is strictly responsible, and when you really don't think you are the responsible party, such words should not be lightly used. That's my view of the matter, in any case.

## The Story behind Ghibli's Going Independent

Ghibli left Tokuma Shoten and went independent in March 2005. Personally I had no complaints about producing films as part of the Tokuma group. As long as we could make films, that was enough. The truth is that, due to various circumstances, Ghibli was forced to strike out on its own.

Just about the time the company was established (1985), I had this conversation with Miya-san.

"Suzuki-san, what are you going to do?"

"What do you mean?"

"Are you going to stay with Tokuma Shoten, or are you going to work with me?"

"I think I'll stay with Tokuma."

"Why would you do that?"

"I want someone else to take responsibility for business management."

"Oh. I see."

To tell the truth, until I had this conversation with Miya-san, I hadn't considered other options. Even talking with him, I simply thought, "Oh, that's a possibility." The fact is, you can't make a decent movie if you are always concerned about money. Having someone else shoulder the burden of managing the company and handling the finances, a separate entity like a president, is the ideal arrangement, I instinctively thought.

In any case, when Ghibli went independent, the banks converged on it like a swarm of locusts. The talk was all about raising a huge amount of capital, from which Ghibli would pay off its debt to the banks. I wanted the company to be capitalized at only 10 million yen. If the capital was too large for us to handle, that would cause us trouble in making the films we wanted. What then would be the purpose of our going independent?

What I disliked most about Ghibli becoming independent was the fact that I might have to serve as president. It might simply have been that almost all the people I knew in that position tended to be penny-pinchers. There is nothing wrong with that, of course. Being in charge of the finances of a company, one will naturally try to reduce expenses—how to cut production costs, how to economize on wages, how to scrimp on a single sheet of paper! This may, in fact, be the most important quality needed by a company president. But for me that would be the cause of tremendous stress.

So my first task at the newly independent Ghibli was to find a president. I broached the subject to a number of people, but none gave an affirmative answer. One commented, "With you and Miyazaki-san there, being president wouldn't be easy." He may have a point, I thought, and so, left with no other choice, I became president of Ghibli.

### Not Being Particular about the Company Name

From the beginning, the name Studio Ghibli became a problem. Until then, it had been the name of one division in the Tokuma group. When the idea of purchasing the name came up, it wasn't greeted with open arms. And it wouldn't be cheap. The whole problem seemed to be more trouble than it was worth. Miya-san said, "Let's just forget the name Ghibli." I was of the same opinion. Neither of us was devoted to the company in that sense. "Do you have any good ideas?" I asked him.

In situations like this, Miya-san doesn't waste time but falls immediately to thinking. What he came up with was "sirocco." I mentioned earlier that "ghibli" was the name for a Saharan wind. Well, sirocco is the name for another wind in the Sahara desert. Since Miya--san and I are quick to act once a decision has been made, we immediately began spreading the news around the new studio.

"We're changing the name of the company."

"What's it going to be?"

"Sirocco."

"Huh!"

Then one of the female staff frankly said, "I don't like it." When I asked why, she said that when answering the phone, Ghibli had some power to it, but Sirocco sounded weak. "It's no good," I thought.

I reported to Miya-san that the new name was not being favorably received and asked, "Don't you have something else?" We struggled with it for a while, but nothing surfaced, so in the end we had to stick with Ghibli.

It seemed that the production staff were more attached to the name Ghibli than anyone else, which reminds me of a story concerning the tie-up with Disney. When the video was released, there was a question from staff: once the tie-up is concluded and a video released, would the Disney logo appear at the beginning of the film? I was somewhat taken aback by the nature of the question, since I myself didn't place much importance in the matter. Why were they being so particular about a name? It wouldn't bother me in the least if the name Ghibli were tossed by the wayside.

## The Importance of Inspiration

The year after Ghibli went independent, Goro Miyazaki debuted as a director with *Tales from Earthsea*. At the time, making him director gave rise to a great deal of faultfinding. How could he possibly direct a work as important as this even though he had never made an animation before? It was unthinkable, and so on. Most of all, Miya-san was absolutely against the idea.

It is a well-known fact that Miya-san is a great fan of Ursula K. Le Guin's *Earthsea* books. When he visited the United States and met the author, he told her frankly that all of his work after *Nausicaä* had been influenced by her writing. In fact, from a very early date he had wanted to do an animated version of *Earthsea*, but when he asked for permission to do so, he didn't get it. It was just about the time that the production of *Howl's Moving Castle* was reaching its busiest stage when, through Le Guin's translator, Masako Shimizu, we learned that Le Guin was personally asking that *Earthsea* be made into a Miyazaki animation. She had seen *Princess Mononoke* and *Spirited Away* and had been very moved. This was good news, and we at once formed a team to take it under consideration. One of the team's pivotal figures was Goro Miyazaki, who was then director of the Ghibli Museum. At the start he wasn't considered for the position of director, but as time passed I began to think he would be a good choice.

In any case, it was very courageous of Goro to undertake the film. After all, his father was the famous Hayao Miyazaki, and he would be debuting as the director of the work that had had the greatest influence on his father's recent films, as Miyazaki himself had publicly declared. The pressure must have been enormous. The film wasn't something that could be approached lightheartedly. Miya-san, who had vehemently opposed the idea at first, finally came around and gave his permission when he learned at a family gathering how determined Goro was.

At first Miya-san wasn't very happy about the idea and told me, "How can you have a person without one iota of experience direct a film? Something must be wrong with you!" But I had a certain idea in the back of my head: it was a line from *Porco Rosso*. When Porco Rosso's plane needs repairs, a young female mechanic, Fio, appears to do the job. When Porco tries to turn her away as being too inexperienced, she asks him, "Which is more important—experience or inspiration?"

Coming to a sudden realization, he answers "Inspiration" and accepts her for the job. To my mind, young Goro's position was much the same. When the film was completed, it was subjected to some pretty severe criticism, but the fact that 6.1 million people viewed it was huge. Even the sharp-tongued Mamoru Oshii praised the film, and the multitalented Shunji Iwai raved about it. Goro was immensely pleased.

## The Future of Ghibli

As of 2008, Ghibli has been in existence for some twenty years. It is still a company where anything might happen. The biggest reason for this is Miya-san: he built a museum, created a kindergarten (opened in 2008), and is oblivious to profit and loss. Takahata-san, working at his own pace, also comes up with a lot of good ideas. This mood of high tension has been continually maintained from the beginning. Miya-san hasn't changed since I first met him, and neither has his way of working. As long as those two are around, the company won't change, I think. The company may disappear one of these days; it may be taken over by someone else. To summarize my thoughts, I will quote something I wrote earlier in "'Sen to Chihiro' wa Dizuni ni katta" ("Spirited Away" Beats Disney).

> *I am often asked my thoughts concerning how to foster the next generation of animators. My answer is this: the best thing that could happen would be for the generation represented by picky people like me and Miya-san to disappear. [Laughs]*
>
> *But having long listened to what Miya-san says, I have the feeling that he wants to do another three films. I'll just have to tag along, I suppose. So Ghibli should be around for at least another ten years. Ghibli has no intention of becoming a global standard like Disney, producing films that can be seen and enjoyed anywhere in the world. What we want to do is to produce films that reflect the age*

*we live in and are universal in theme, the result of Miya-san's and my everyday conversations and our quest for technical excellence.*

February 2008 saw some good news both for Ghibli and for myself. The former chairman of Walt Disney Japan, Koji Hoshino, agreed to become president of Ghibli, officially taking over for me on February 1. We had known each other since 1994 when he proposed that Disney serve as a video distributor for Ghibli films, an idea that was realized in 1996. Learning that he would be leaving Disney, I proposed that he assume the presidency of Ghibli in May 2007. Following my established rule, I didn't ask again after that once. I always leave the decision up to the other party and just patiently wait. About three months later he gave me an affirmative answer.

Now, in this new organization, I could concentrate on being a producer and leave the management of the company in his hands. At the press conference he referred to something I had mentioned to him and said, "I want to maintain Ghibli as it has been up until now, but that doesn't mean I will avoid conflict. I want to act as a catalyst in producing a new kind of chemistry with the staff."

## Your Favorite Film

I am often asked, of all the films I have worked on, which is my favorite. I think this is a rather silly question, because for anyone doing creative work the answer is obvious: their favorite film is the one they are working on at the moment.

What is over is over and done. That's why I never rewatch films from the past. When a film is in production, I watch it any number of times from different angles, and that is enough. Usually I look at the sections called rushes, which are unedited scenes made for previewing purposes. It is not often that I watch a film from beginning to end. When I'm done working on a something, somehow I get the feeling,

"I really need to stay away from this film for a while." So I don't watch it anymore. My mind has already moved on.

This reminds me of the dialogue I had with Mamoru Oshii (mentioned earlier), in which I said the following near the beginning of the dialogue.

> *Suzuki: As a matter of fact, just recently I watched* Nausicaä of the Valley of the Wind *for the first time in twenty years. What I felt on re-seeing the film was that Nausicaä was attempting to save the wounded earth with her own hands. This was a heavy burden. The works of that time, such as* Space Battleship Yamato, *all had grandiose themes. But Miya-san's more recent works are different. For example, Ashitaka, the protagonist of* Princess Mononoke, *sets off on his journey for very personal reasons.*
> (*Shinshun anime taidan: Suzuki Toshio vs. Oshii Mamoru* [New Year's Anime Dialogue: Toshio Suzuki vs. Mamoru Oshii]; *Yomiuri* newspaper, 2004).

Twenty years had in fact passed since I had last seen *Nausicaä*. That's a long time. But that gap enabled me to read the times in which the film was made. That is, I could see that the themes of films had shifted dramatically toward personal concerns. That is the definite impression I got from rewatching *Nausicaä.*

Aside from that, I think I would like to name my favorite films on my deathbed. After all, there is still the future ahead of us.

## *Ponyo* Is Great!

At the moment I am having a great time working as producer on *Ponyo.*

In a sense, Miya-san spent more time on the preparation stage of *Ponyo* than any film since *Nausicaä*. He started thinking about it immediately after the release of *Howl* in November 2004 and commenced production in October 2006, a period of almost two years. Given that, until then, this stage of working out the finer points of the plan had taken a minimum of three months and a maximum of six, *Ponyo* was in a class by itself.

One of the motivations for starting *Ponyo* was a conversation I had with Miya-san just after *Howl* was finished.

"Suzuki-san, what should we do next?"

"How about something for younger children?"

"Why's that?"

"In *Howl* the exchanges between Calcifer, Markl, and Sophie were really well done. You don't often see scenes of that caliber in films for children."

Miya-san was very pleased to hear that. At first we thought of basing the story on *Iyaiya-en* (No-No Academy) by the children's writer Rieko Nakagawa, though in the end the theme of the story changed for various reasons.

Another catalyst for making *Ponyo* was a company trip. It was exactly on the day *Howl* was released that we were invited to visit a harbor town on the Seto Inland Sea. At first Miya-san was not very eager to go, but once there, he really liked the place. Later he would rent a house and spend two months there. He always develops an interest in towns he has visited or places he has resided in for a time. It was his trip to Yakushima that produced the image for *Nausicaä*. His memories of Sweden influenced *Kiki's Delivery Service*. That's how the backdrop for *Ponyo* became a harbor on the Seto Inland Sea.

It was at that time that Miya-san began reading Soseki Natsume, and was much taken with Sosuke, the protagonist of *Mon* (The Gate). In the novel Sosuke lives at the "bottom" of a cliff, but in the film Miya-san changed this to "on" a cliff. The five-year-old protagonist of the film retained the same name as in Soseki's work. Miya-san said he became fixated on Soseki and the time the novelist had time spent in London as a student on a government scholarship. He wanted to see the paintings in the Tate Gallery that had so impressed Soseki, especially Millet's *Ophelia* based on Shakespeare's *Hamlet.* He actually arranged to go to England, combining the trip with another errand. There he ruminated over the character of the drowning woman.

All of these factors were taken in by Miya-san and mixed and fermented. *Ponyo* was the first Miyazaki film in which such careful preparations were made, where everything was woven together and thought out in great detail.

*Ponyo* was also the first film in which all the drawing was done by hand—not a single instance of computer graphics. In particular, Miya-san enjoyed drawing the waves. He wanted to devise a new way of expressing waves and the sea. He didn't leave this work to others; he did it himself. He had returned to the roots of animation. At one point he said, "I am going to teach my son more about making animation." Concerning *Tales from Earthsea*, directed by his son Goro, he said, "It's a good, straightforward presentation," but he still felt there was more he could teach Goro about creative directing. That, at any rate, seemed to be what was on his mind.

In any event, no matter how old he gets, Miya-san continues to rise to new challenges. It's quite impressive. Thinking that this will certainly be a Miyazaki masterpiece, as a producer I feel the excitement well up in me.

## Loving My Work, Loving the People I Have Worked with

In the end what I have enjoyed most is interacting with people. There is nothing greater than interacting with people at a profound level, to work surrounded by people you like. What more can one ask? It is also good for your mental well-being. I met up with people like Miya-san, Takahata-san, and President Tokuma, and somehow arrived at the present day, enjoying myself along the way. Of course, there are many other people I like.

Given the nature of my work as a producer, it is only natural that I should come into contact with a lot of people. But I don't think of this as merely business. It is not an intra-company relationship, but a person-to-person relationship. I work with companies that would ordinarily be considered deadly rivals, such as Dentsu and Hakuhodo, Lawson and 7-Eleven. However, when a particular person leaves one of these companies, there is no telling how the relationship with that company will be affected. Ghibli has interacted with Disney because of Koji Hoshino; their present relationship is due to him. The relationship with Pixar is due solely to the presence of John Lasseter.

I spend time with these people because I enjoy it. For example, there is a Spielberg producer named Kathleen Kennedy who I have known for something like ten years. She is a very charming person and an interesting conversationalist. When I visit the United States, we always have dinner together. When she comes to Japan, I take her to whatever sights she wants to see. We frequently exchange emails. Our relationship has continued in this way without once talking about work. However, just recently the subject of work came up, in connection with Hoshino-san becoming the president of Ghibli. As you might expect of Hoshino, he wanted to expand the company's activities on a worldwide scale. On the spur of the moment, so to speak, he approached Kathleen about handling Ghibli films in North America. She was delighted with the idea and is now eagerly considering the possibilities. This development is a fortunate happenstance, however; not something that was planned beforehand.

Thinking back about it, I believe this episode directly reflects some important aspects of my general approach to work. Putting aside the issue of short-term goals, I have never set up a long-term goal and devoted myself wholeheartedly to achieving it. This undoubtedly has something to do with my notion that thinking of goals without considering interaction with people is meaningless. So when I am asked what Ghibli's management or advertising strategy is, I want to say, "God, give me a break!" The word "strategy" doesn't suit me, and I never use it. As I wrote in "In Place of a Preface" at the beginning of this book, I concentrate all my energy on the issue at hand, on a goal that is just slightly ahead. To me the word "strategy" means tactics, considering all possibilities, testing all hypotheses for solutions. I do this because I enjoy it. I love trying to figure problems out. At the center of my thinking are, invariably, "people." Making sure no one drops out, doing my best to persuade people who are in opposition—these are the ironclad rules I have adhered to. The best work is produced when everyone is of the same mind, when all are enjoying what they are doing.

This often puzzles people, but I have never felt deeply disappointed or frustrated in my job. Doing the type of work I do, without any long-term goals, it is only natural that I should never feel frustrated or disappointed. Once, on April 6, 2006, when I appeared on the NHK General TV series called *Purofesshonaru shigoto no ryugi* (The Ways of Professionals; a.k.a. The Professionals), this caused a bit of a problem. The theme of the episode was "Frustration and the Recovery from Frustration," and when I said I never felt frustrated, they were unable to develop a coherent story. I racked my brains trying to think of something, but failed. [Laughs]

In fact, I have never thought that I wanted to be a certain type of person or hoped to become famous at something. Maybe that's the reason I have never considered anyone to be a rival. I don't think of people in that way. As I said earlier, it is simply a matter of working with people I like in a job that I like. It's as simple as that.

Among my favorite words is *doraku* (lit. the path of pleasure), which can be translated as "hobby" or "pastime." The first book I ever published was called *Eiga doraku* (*eiga* meaning "movies"; 2005), a title I conceived myself. *Doraku* is really an excellent word. It implies not exerting oneself to become a certain something, but enjoying each spontaneous moment with someone one likes. This is truly, I think, to tread a path of pleasure. In fact, it may be that *doraku* enables one to see the world more clearly. What I have written up to this point is my *shigoto doraku* (*shigoto* meaning "work"), my way of mixing work and pleasure.

In the end I can't help but feel that I owe my character to my parents, and to my mother in particular. This year (2008) she turned eighty-five, and she is a very tough person, typical of the generation that lived through the war. To conclude this chapter I would like to relate two personal episodes.

One took place when I had just become the vice editor-in-chief of the magazine *Animage* at Tokuma Shoten. I called my mother and told her the good news. No sooner were the words out of my mouth than she fairly shouted at me, "What a stupid thing to do! Why would you want to be promoted? Don't let them take advantage of you. By giving you a title they only want to make you work harder." Then she went on, "There are only two important things in this life. One is your health." This was easy enough to understand, especially since she used a familiar phrase in our shared Nagoya dialect. "If you work too hard, you'll ruin your health," she said, continuing: "The most important thing of all is to be alert and keep your wits about you. Don't be a fool and just plug away at your job." What a terrible mother! [Laughs] But thanks to her, I developed the habit of taking an objective view of my position in life. That was very important. I might have an inflated opinion of myself because of the new title, but I shouldn't let that fool me. Far from praising me, she had gotten angry.

The other episode involves my mother when she was in elementary school. She said that the emperor visited Nagoya, and all the students lined up to greet him. At that time the emperor was considered a "living god," and the principal warned the students not to raise their heads and look directly at him; anyone who did so would go blind. After all, he was a living god, and laying one's eyes on him would mean the loss of your sight. When she came near the end of her story, I asked her, "So what happened?"

"I looked at him, of course," she said. "But I didn't go blind."

In any event, she is my mother, and even though her memory is not what it used to be, it was this kind of spirit that formed the bedrock of my life.

# 8 The Future Opens Up to the Steady and Steadfast

## Always Think in the Present Tense

September 6, 2013, following the press conference at which Miyazaki announced his retirement. Although they had worked together for more than thirty years, this was the first time for Suzuki and Miyazaki to shake hands. (Photo provided by *Asahi Shimbun*.)

**Hayao Miyazaki**

---

I want to work for at least ten more years. I want to continue to work as long as I can drive and commute back and forth between my home and the Studio. I set the target for now for at least ten years.

It could be shorter, but life will decide, so ten years is just an aim.

I wanted to make feature animation, and I have made many, but I could not stop the gap between films from growing. What I mean is, I was getting slower.

It took five years to complete *The Wind Rises*. Would it take six years, or seven even, for the next film? The Studio cannot wait for me, and I will be using up my time in my seventies.

Besides feature animation, I have a lot of things I would like to do—or at least try. I also have some things I must do—new exhibitions at the Ghibli Museum is one example—and there are other challenges to tackle.

Most of the things I will do will not cause trouble for the Studio although I will continue to cause trouble for my family just like now.

So, I asked the Studio to exclude me from its plans.

I will be free. But my lifestyle will remain same, using the same route to commute to the Studio every day. My dream is to rest on Saturdays, but I must figure out whether that will be possible once I start.

Thank you very much.

Official Retirement Statement, September 4, 2013

---

What follows is a new chapter added to the first edition of this book. The original edition brought the story up to just before the release of *Ponyo on the Cliff by the Sea* in 2008. Six years have passed since then. Ghibli has commemorated its thirtieth anniversary, and I am facing a turning point in my life. How did things reach this juncture?

## Miya-san's Five-Year Plan

*Ponyo*, which was successfully released in July 2008, drew an audience of 12 million people and grossed box office revenues of 15.5 billion yen. Just as we were contemplating what to do next, Miya-san suddenly produced a new idea. "I have come up with a midrange five-year plan for Ghibli. Let's have the younger animators do two films in three years' time and follow that with a full-length blockbuster film over the next two years." In other words, his plan called for three films over five years. My first reaction to this idea was astonishment. Personally I had always thought of each individual film as an end in itself. I had no interest in long-term planning. What crossed my mind was: "Does this mean that Miya-san wants to have two films produced before he actually does one himself?"

At the time I thought it might be interesting to work on two films that were not specifically directed by Miya-san over a period of three years. These two films became *Karigurashi no Arietti* (Arrietty, 2010) and *Kokuriko-zaka kara* (From Up on Poppy Hill, 2011).

## From Director-Centered to Planning-Centered Films

Broadly speaking, up to this point the modus operandi at Ghibli had been for Hayao Miyazaki and Isao Takahata to take turns producing films. The projects existed because the directors existed. The director's wishes were paramount in whatever was done. It might be called a director-centered system. This time, however, things would be different.

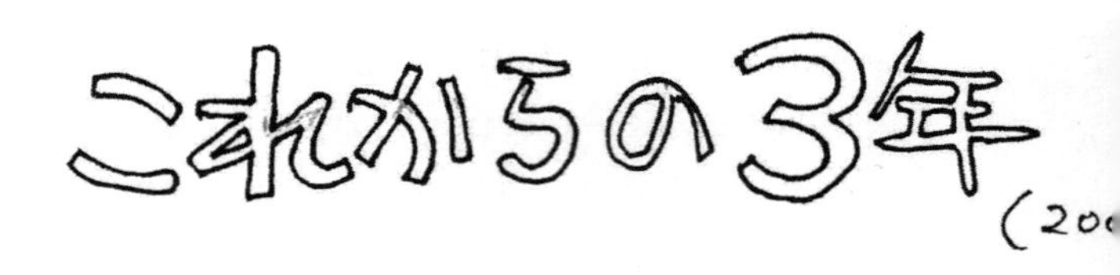


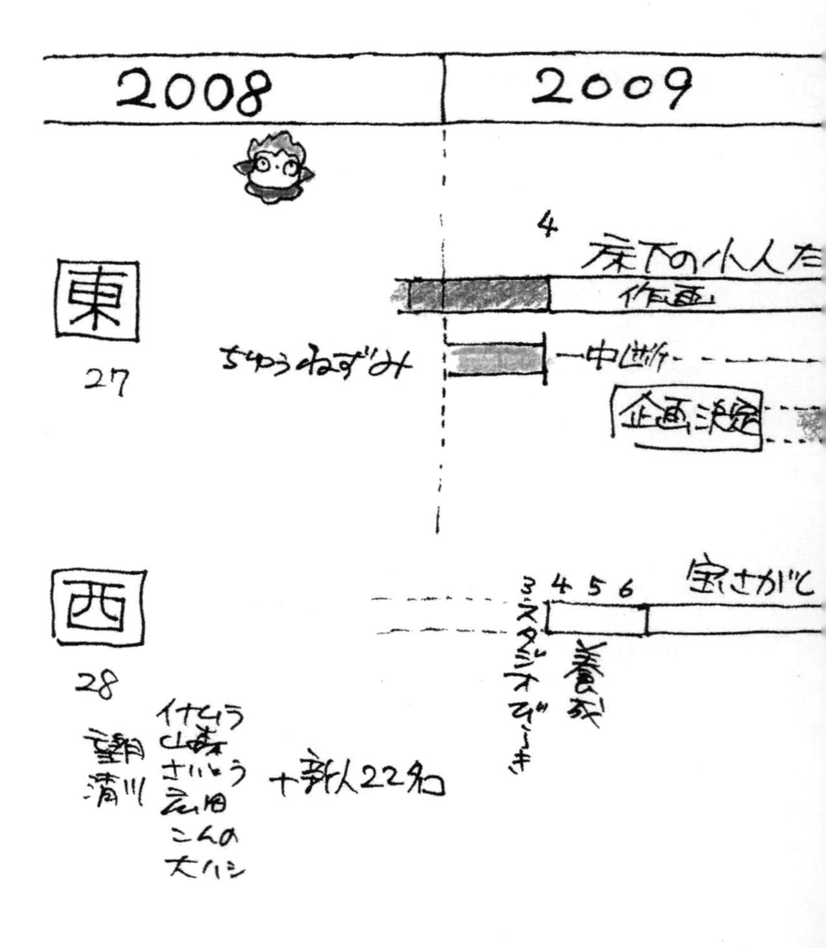


November 2008, just after the release of *Ponyo*. This memo, inscribed "The Next Three Years" in Miyazaki's own hand, was produced by Miyazaki to outline his five-year plan. It resulted in *Arrietty*, *From Up on Poppy Hill*, and *The Wind Rises*.

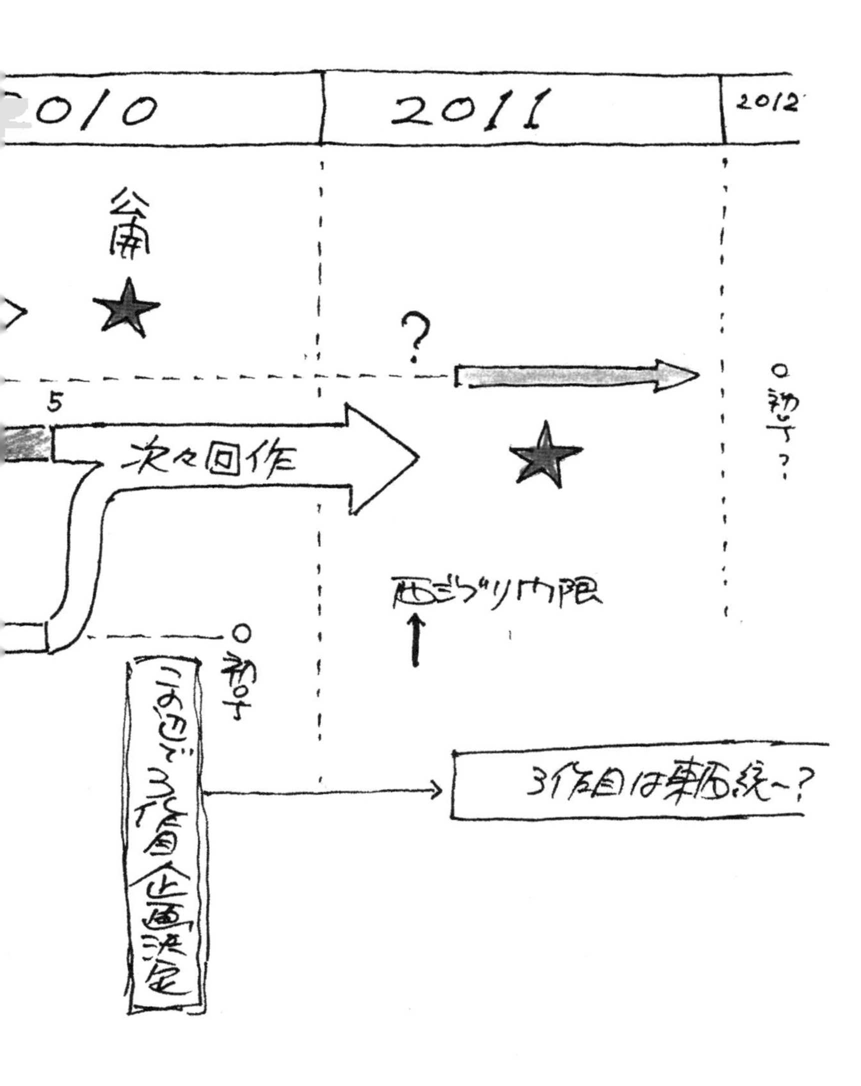
2011
公開
5
次々回作
?
初号
この辺で3作目企画決定

The planning and even the scenario would be provided by the producer. The film would be made by the director on this basis, in what might be called a planning-centered system. Miya-san said this was fine with him, and I agreed.

So what kind of films would they be? The ideas for doing *Arrietty* and *Poppy Hill* were both Miya-san's. *Arrietty*, which was settled on in the summer of 2008, would be based on *The Borrowers*, a novel by Mary Norton. As a matter of fact, in their younger days Takahata and Miya-san had considered this book for animation. The story showed how the human world appeared in the eyes of a family of tiny people. While this view of the book was undoubtedly true, when I read it, I was particularly struck by the notion of the tiny people borrowing from human beings what they needed in their daily lives. The Borrowers don't possess any magical powers; they don't have any money; they are just very small. How will they survive from day to day? The answer to this question is: they will live each day to the utmost of their ability. They are happy, much as human families used to be. This theme, if nothing else, seemed to have present-day ramifications, which is the reason I suggested that the word *karigurashi* (lit. a borrowed living) be added to *Arietti* to form the Japanese title: *Karigurashi no Arietti* (Arrietty's Borrowed Life). Miya-san liked the idea.

Next came *From Up on Poppy Hill*. We were in the midst of making *Arrietty* toward the end of 2009 when Miya-san suddenly suggested doing *Poppy Hill*. It was to be based on a girls' manga of the same name. Years ago we had taken this manga under consideration when discussing the possibility of doing an animation based on a manga for girls. The project hadn't been realized, but now, when I heard Miya-san's proposition, I began to think that this was the right moment for such a movie. In a sense, it was a modern version of the film *Aoi sanmyaku* (Blue Mountain Range), which had played a large part in energizing postwar Japanese. In our day and age, I thought, there was a need for a movie like this.

As it turned out, *Arrietty* and *Poppy Hill*, as Ghibli films, presented a sharp contrast. In fact, you could say they were exact opposites in orientation. *Arrietty* featured tiny people, so it could easily be treated as a fantasy and was not that different from the usual Ghibli production. *Poppy Hill*, on the other hand, was about an ordinary high-school student. The setting was Yokohama in 1963, the year before the Tokyo Olympics. It contained not one iota of fantasy. Almost coincidentally, we ended up making two films, one on top of the other, that shared nothing in common.

## The Emergence of Hiromasa Yonebayashi (Maro) and the Re-emergence of Goro Miyazaki

Once the planning was completed, the next problem was who the directors should be. We hadn't discussed the directors at all. While we agreed that they should be young, who exactly were they to be?

First was *Arrietty*. There wasn't much time left when Miya-san showed up and said, "Suzuki-san, what are we going to do about the director? You'll have overall responsibility, right?" Without my really thinking, the word "Maro" popped out of my mouth. For a moment Miya-san looked puzzled, as if he had been blindsided. And for good reason: Maro (Hiromasa Yonebayashi) was Ghibli's best animator. If he became a director, Miya-san would be left without Maro's services for his own films. But he didn't let this faze him for long. Almost instantly, as if to brush off any second thoughts, he said, "Good. Let's call Maro right now."

Maro was thrown for a loop. He loved his job, and the thought of directing had probably never entered his mind. But then, out of the blue, Miya-san was telling him, "This is the next project. You're the director." It took him a little while to get used to the idea, but in any case the matter had been decided. To tell the truth, this was a bit of a risk. Maro himself had never aspired to be a director, and he had no experience. But he proved much more capable than expected, something I will touch on later.

As for *Poppy Hill*, Goro Miyazaki was named director. He had been eager to make another film. Once upon a time I had told him, "A film director can't be picky. You have to take on whatever comes your way, regardless of personal preference." He understood this, and was prepared to do his best. Miya-san had always said that a director's second film was the real test. I'm sure that Goro felt the pressure.

One of Goro's outstanding qualities is his ability to bring a group together. When making a film, one is sometimes compelled to push people rather hard. In this atmosphere Goro is good at creating moments of relaxation. I got this impression very strongly during the production of *Tales from Earthsea* (2006). Neither Miya-san nor Takahata-san possesses this knack.

### Scriptwriting: The Contribution of Keiko Niwa

Since *Arrietty* was to be a planning-centered film, the script was especially important. The screenplay would be done by Miya-san in combination with someone else. The question was who the other person would be. The individual who came to mind was Keiko Niwa. She is now working in the editorial department of a certain publishing company, but before that she had been at Tokuma Shoten under me during my *Animage* period. Before entering Tokuma she had studied at Shochiku's scenario research center, distinguishing herself so resoundingly that she was considered a prodigy. I had asked her to do the script for Ghibli's 1993 TV special *Umi ga kikoeru* (The Ocean Waves), and I remember being impressed by her work.

Miya-san, however, was not an easy person to work with. He paid little attention to overall structure but focused on minute details. The story developed like a game of word association. Traditional Japanese ways of structuring a story, such as *kishotenketsu*, played no part at all.

There would be a lot of places that just didn't make sense. And he had so many ideas that it was difficult to fit them all into the allotted time. But it wasn't just this stream of ideas that was the problem; just as you thought something had been accomplished, he would come up with some entirely different thoughts the next day. This would drive most screenwriters up the wall, but Keiko Niwa found it interesting. She seemed to find his thinking process—the thinking of a genius—immensely intriguing, and she loved working with him.

When the time came for *Poppy Hill*, we naturally asked Niwa to do the script with Miya-san. This time I took a hand in the overall scriptwriting process, but Niwa was absolutely phenomenal. She was a perfect match for Miya-san. After the daily meetings were over, she would immediately sum up what Miya-san had said. Sometimes he would turn everything on its head, but she remained unflustered and rewrote the script any number of times. This was undoubtedly the first time for a script of Miya-san's to be done in this way.

## Maro as a Director

There are some directors who want to brand their films with their own personalities, to have a hand in every single detail, much like a novelist. Miya-san exemplifies this type. Maro, on the other hand, is more of a stage manager than a director. The fact is, even if two theater directors are using the same script, the results will be different. The difference between a director and a stage manager is something like that. The stage manager brings out the best in each role, lets the actors perform as they please, and concentrates on manipulating the script for greater effect. Maro is this type of director.

The main problem for Miya-san in this case was deciding who would produce the storyboards from his script. This would determine the character of the movie. I discussed this point at various times with Maro. If Miya-san supervised this aspect of the film, it would be hard for Maro to preserve his independence. I told him, "I recommend that you do the storyboards yourself."

"Yes," he responded, "that was my intention."

The two of us went to see Miya-san, and Maro told him that he would be doing the storyboards. Miya-san said, "Okay. You're a grown man now. If you say you're going to do it all yourself, I won't offer advice or lend a helping hand." But Miya-san is not the type to keep his thoughts to himself. It was as plain as day that he would want to put in his two cents and get involved. At my recommendation, Maro holed up in a room in a nearby apartment building, working on the storyboards. His whereabouts were kept secret. This began to eat away at Miya-san, and he caused a commotion about it: "Where in heaven's name has Maro gone off to?"

Looking at the finished film, I can clearly see the individual differences between the two men. Take the character Arrietty, for example. If it were up to Miya-san, he would make her the type of girl who acts before she thinks. But in Maro's version, Arrietty always thinks before she acts. This is a huge difference. It may have something to do with personal preference in female types. The romantic scenes were particularly interesting. In Miya-san's work, the moment a boy and a girl meet they are attracted to one another at once, 100 percent. There is no maneuvering or calculation. And the attraction is simultaneously accompanied by physical contact. With Maro, on the other hand, the various stages of attraction are clearly differentiated.

## An Average of Five Seconds Becomes Four

Here is an incident that occurred during the production of *Poppy Hill.* Completing the script had taken longer than expected, leaving Goro with little time to spare for the storyboards and fine-tuned adjustments. When, at long last, twenty-five minutes of storyboarding were finished, we checked it with the leica reel, still images arranged in sequence with recorded material. What we saw left us speechless. The tempo was wrong, and the heroine too gloomy. Goro practically held his head in his hands. On a whim I replayed the leica reel at 1.3 times the normal speed. As a result, the tempo picked up, and even the heroine changed for the better. When I pointed this out to Goro, he looked at me rather wide-eyed and said, "Oh, you're right."

At Ghibli the usual shot lasts five seconds. Of course, there are longer and shorter shots, but this is about the average. Compared to the typical animation, five seconds is rather long. I haven't done a careful calculation of all the various types of animation that exist, but I think the average must be about three or four seconds. With the longer shots, drawing the background to the story proves a chore. If five seconds is reduced to four, not only is the tempo improved, but productivity is enhanced. In any event, time is crucial, and there is not much of it. But if both tempo and productivity can be improved at one fell swoop, two birds are killed with one stone. The fact that this artifice proves so effective is related to the nature of the film. There are two types of film: one in which the story is simple but the means of expression is complex; the other in which the story is complicated but the means of expression is simple. *Poppy Hill* falls into the latter category.

The principal attraction of *Poppy Hill* is, of course, its heroine. The reason she seemed rather gloomy at first was due to the scenario, which Miya-san noticed and fixed. Taking this revision, Goro assailed it tooth and nail and did a splendid job. He didn't produce a sweet little girl who seems to be fishing for compliments on how cute she looks; he produced a character who is unconcerned about what other people think of her, who is as straight as an arrow. He makes you think there might be such a girl living nearby. That's the kind of character Umi is, a modern girl through and through.

## Looking Back on *Arrietty* and *Poppy Hill*

*Arrietty* was released on July 17, 2010. It drew an audience of 7.65 million people and grossed 9.25 billion yen in box office revenue. *Poppy Hill* was released on July 16, 2011, drew an audience of 3.55 million people, and grossed 4.46 billion yen. As the producer I considered them both big successes.

In box office terms *Poppy Hill* garnered only half the revenue of *Arrietty*. One reason for this was the fact that it had no fantasy elements and was therefore different from the style Ghibli had fostered over the years. It was an entirely different type of movie. In one sense it was a risky experiment; we weren't sure how viewers would react. In fact, at a gathering of concerned parties, I told them plainly that, ordinarily, this film would only be shown at independent theaters, but we wanted to challenge that perception, and they should view the film with that in mind. After seeing it, Dwango's Nobuo Kawakami remarked, "It seems to be lacking in pizzazz." We have to remember, though, the Great East Japan earthquake had occurred that March, and people were not in the mood to go to the theater. Still, it had the best box office earnings among Japanese films for that year. In my opinion it performed remarkably well.

In any event, the first half of Miya-san's five-year plan had come to an end. *Arrietty* under Maro and *Poppy Hill* under Goro had shown they could meet the expectations of the general public. From the perspective of fantasy, as mentioned earlier, the two films were exact opposites. *Arrietty* seemed to be a return to Ghibli's nostalgic past. Some said this was what Ghibli should be, but there were also those who said *Poppy Hill* was their favorite Ghibli film. Both reactions were highly welcome, and in fact this favorable response seems to have created a broader fan base. In that sense, *Arrietty* and *Poppy Hill* proved their worth. I can't help feeling very satisfied, a certain sense of accomplishment.

### *The Wind Rises:* Why Miya-san Was Against It

The grand finale to the five-year plan would, naturally, be directed by Miya-san. In 2010 I began urging him to make preparations. Actually, what he wanted to do was another movie like *Ponyo*, a sort of *Ponyo 2*. He wanted to do something to please his grandson, who was the apple of his eye. This is so typical of Miya-san.

In all likelihood this would be Miya-san's last film. Working side by side with him for thirty-five years, there was one thing that preyed on my mind. If Miya-san were to make a film about war, what kind of film would it be? He had a detailed knowledge of war-related matters, and loved drawing fighter planes and tanks. On the other hand, he was a great advocate of world peace, and he even participated in antiwar demonstrations. I wanted him to direct a movie that resolved this seeming contradiction. Just once he should confront the issue head-on, I thought. I was aware that from around 2008 he had been planning a manga series on Jiro Horikoshi, the designer of the Zero fighter. The series, titled *The Wind Rises*, eventually got started in a hobbyist model magazine. In the summer of 2010 I suggested we make it into a film.

His response was decisive, pulling no punches. "Something must be wrong with you, Suzuki-san. I'm doing this as a pastime. A film is out of the question." He also said, "Animations should be made for children, not adults." Up until now Miya-san had always valued my opinion, and he continued to agonize over the matter.

Of all the Ghibli projects up to that point, *The Wind Rises* was the first not to be quickly green-lighted. Miya-san just didn't want to do it, no matter what. But I didn't give in. After all, one of the functions of a producer is to act as a pesky critic. Near the end of 2010 the "go" sign was finally given. After that, Miya-san was all action. He had barely started the storyboards at the beginning of the New Year, but by March he had reached the point where Jiro and Naoko meet.

Partway through the project, there were places that deviated from the original concept. One was a scene depicting a dogfight between planes. Since the subject of the film was fighter planes, you would ordinarily expect there to be a scene showing planes engaged in close combat. I myself was of that opinion, and I was particularly interested in how this was going to be accomplished. Miya-san, being of the same mind, tried various approaches, but none of them reached a level that satisfied him. The matter of age may have been a significant consideration here, but in any case he couldn't draw what he wished. One day he came and said he wanted to abandon the scene. This decision showed Miya-san at his best as a craftsman. Of course, he could have produced a conventional, run-of-the-mill fight scene, but that went against his grain. It went against his integrity as an animator. I could understand his feelings and concurred wholeheartedly.

### How to Attract an Audience

The following is an excerpt from Miya-san's project proposal for *The Wind Rises*, in which he outlined the artistic intent of the film.

> *I want to portray a devoted individual who pursued his dream head on. Dreams possess an element of madness, and such poison must not be concealed. Yearning for something too beautiful can ruin you. Swaying towards beauty may come at a price. Jiro will be battered and defeated, his design career cut short. Nonetheless, Jiro was an individual of preeminent originality and talent. This is what we will strive to portray in this film.*

The project was officially accepted, and promotion was begun. However, the first reaction of the distributor, Toho, was far from positive. It was different from the usual Miyazaki film, they said. It was a war movie, so the audience would be largely male; and it wasn't a family film. Some said that the most that could be expected in terms of box office returns was 6 billion yen, not even half as much as *Ponyo*.

No matter what, I didn't want this figure to become the film's box office target. The only thing that could maintain Miya-san's status as a popular creator and entertainer was box office revenue. Privately my thoughts were on breaking the 10-billion-yen mark. No Japanese movie since *Ponyo* had reached that level. I set that figure as my goal, come hell or high water.

Before actual production of the film had started, Miya-san came to ask my opinion. He was debating whether to focus on the friendship between Jiro and Caproni or on the love story involving Jiro and Naoko. "What do you think?" he asked. My answer was, "Why don't you mix them together?" In other words, the first half would be "friendship," the second half "love." But given Toho's initial reaction, we would have to be careful in how this was presented. The friendship aspect would have to be restrained and the love aspect brought to the fore. I focused the advertising on a female audience. Then we did something that broke all conventional rules, something never done before. We made a four-minute trailer and showed it at theaters. It focused strictly on the love-story aspect of the film.

Perhaps this trailer had some effect, for the film ultimately drew a great many female viewers. Incidentally, what made me think, "Wow, this is the dawn of a new era," was the fact that young women empathized with Jiro's way of life and young men admired Naoko. It was inconceivable. That such a thing should transpire was simply mind-boggling.

The success of the film was enhanced by two subsidiary factors. One was that we were able to use *Hikoki Gumo* performed by Yumi Arai (Yuming) as the theme song. The other was that the voice of Jiro was done by Hideaki Anno, the director of *Shinseiki Evangerion* (Neon Genesis Evangelion). These two factors were hugely newsworthy in themselves. In dubbing the last scene, Anno's off-record reaction was

Studio Ghibli during the ADR session for *The Wind Rises*. From left to right: Toshio Suzuki, Miori Takimoto (voice of Naoko), Hideaki Anno (voice of Jiro Horikoshi), and Hayao Miyazaki.

especially interesting. Originally Naoko was to call out to Jiro, "Please come." After a good deal of agonizing over this last line, Miya-san changed it to "You must live." Anno was immensely pleased with the change. Over the microphone he said, "This is the best last scene of all Miya-san's films." Miya-san simply replied, "Thank you."

The result was a box office of 12 billion yen. This was the first film to top 10 billion yen in Japan since *Ponyo* five years earlier, even counting foreign films. Everyone involved in the film was immensely pleased, but what was most surprising of all was their re-evaluation of my work. Prerelease scuttlebutt had been harsh, but now they said things like, "To break the 10 billion mark with a film like that, quite an accomplishment" or "He's a money-maker, that's for sure." [Laughs]

### What Was the Reception Abroad?

How would the film be received by foreign viewers? The first reaction came from the Venice International Film Festival. *The Wind Rises* was nominated to take part in the competition, but its overall assessment was not particularly high. As I learned later, some members of the jury were of the opinion that in places the film supported the war effort, and that seemed to be a big factor in lowering its evaluation. Alas, this is what I had feared. Miya-san's means of expression were so Japanese that they didn't reveal his true antiwar sentiments. What a pity.

The American reaction, however, was different. There are film critics' associations throughout the United States, and animation is one of the categories they take under consideration. Their evaluation of *The Wind Rises* was rather high. Moreover, the work as a whole was seen as being antiwar. The Venetian and American reactions were quite the opposite.

The American view was partly due to the influence of Pixar's John Lasseter, I think. As soon as the film was finished, he came all the way to Japan to see it. He told Miya-san that it was a beautiful love story.

When interviewed on TV, he spoke only of the love story aspect, but after the interview was over, he had this to say: "A technological advancement can change a whole age and bring a country to ruin. This film is a quiet protest against war." Then there was the Spielberg producer Kathleen Kennedy. She went immediately to see the film. She liked it so much that she watched it twice in succession. Her husband, Frank Marshall, also a Spielberg producer, recommended the film to all his acquaintances in the film industry. These kind words by John Lasseter, Kathy, and Frank led to the film winning awards from many American critics circles and played, I believe, a significant role in the success of the film.

In Asia the reception was more complex due to the subject matter. Korean journalists were invited to Ghibli to see the film, and Miya-san also held a press conference. The journalists' reaction can largely be summed up as follows: "Why did you make such a wonderful movie with the designer of the Zero fighter as the protagonist?" This question was asked notwithstanding the fact that all of them were shedding tears at the end. Miya-san didn't have a ready answer. The Chinese reaction was even blunter; we were told straight out that the film could not be shown in China. Interestingly, however, we were further informed that while the film could not be released in theaters out of political considerations, there shouldn't be the least problem in releasing DVDs. We were told this as plain as day. In the end, China is a very practical country.

## Takahata's View

Near the end of 2013 Miya-san, Takahata, and I held a trialogue in the magazine *Bungei Shunju* (February issue, 2014), the first involving the three of us. Takahata had the following to say about *The Wind Rises.*

> *Much like the majority of the female audience, I thought that* The Wind Rises *was a love story involving Jiro Horikoshi and Naoko,*

*and I accepted it as that. But I have a reservation, if I may. Near the end of the film there is the scene showing a desolate field of felled Zero fighters, but I couldn't help feeling that before this scene there should have been something about what really happened during the war, even if depicted objectively.... It wasn't just a matter of the Zero fighters being reduced to rack and ruin; an enormous number of people had died. Aside from Japanese above a certain age, there are many younger people who don't understand what happened during the war. I wanted that to be shown, in one form or another. But I thought at the time that you must have given this a lot of thought, Miya-san. There is no way you couldn't have."*

The truth is that I had already heard Takahata's views of the film on several occasions. He once said that of all Miya-san's recent films this was the one he could watch with the least reservation. The reason he gave was that there is nothing in the story that strains credulity. For Takahata this plays a big part in his assessment criteria. Then there is the character of Jiro himself. At that time in history it was virtually impossible for most people to decry the war. In order to live a life of any sincerity, their only option was to earnestly pursue the work that was in front of them. In that sense, Jiro is representative of the great mass of Japanese people of that time. Then there is Miya-san's appealing depiction of minor characters, something he is especially good at. Kurokawa (Jiro's boss) and the girl Kayo are particularly well done and typical of Miya-san. Et cetera, et cetera.

Prefacing his comments with a "but," Takahata also said that the situation in Japan in 1935, when the Zero was being manufactured, was entirely different from that in 1945. This should have been made explicit in the film. Otherwise, the nature of war doesn't come across. This is something that Takahata had been saying from the beginning, and it was no surprise that it should emerge in the trialogue.

During the discussion Miya-san said that he had, of course,

thought about it, but since the Zero was in operation throughout the war, the story would have become too long if he had tried to cover the entire period. Aside from that, there were a large number of records and testimonies about the war that would have to be considered. He didn't want the film to be seen as an ill-conceived justification for the war, he said. That's why he intentionally didn't cover the whole period. Takahata, however, still wasn't convinced. But when Miya-san said, "Even if I depicted the entire war, Jiro's basic nature as the designer of the Zero would stay exactly the same," Takahata responded, "I can see that," and fell into agreement.

## The In-house Announcement of Miya-san's Retirement

During the production of *The Wind Rises* Miya-san began to say that this would be his last film. The film was completed on June 19, 2013, and it was a few days afterward, I think, that I went to ascertain his thinking. "Is this really your last film?" I asked. He answered, "Oh, yes. This is the last." Since Miya-san is the type of person who can't follow through on a decision unless he makes it public, he wanted to hold a press conference right away, the sooner the better. "I don't think that's a good idea," I replied. "If you announce your retirement just as the film is being released, it might be interpreted as mere promotion. You should make the announcement after things have settled down."

But Miya-san is not what you would call a patient person. "When would that be?" he asked. I said, "We should have a breather after summer, so maybe September." He answered, "You mean I have to wait that long?"

If Miya-san was going to retire, there was one huge problem that had to be faced—the fate of Ghibli, the studio that had been created for Miya-san's films. With his stepping down, what would happen to the staff? For the time being, should we give up making films with permanently employed people? If we decided to make a new film, should we hire staff just for that film. But that would put the people we had worked with for so long in an awful position, and there would be problems in assigning individuals to serve as directors in order to maintain the present system. I discussed these matters with Miya-san.

In any case, before a public announcement could be made, we would have to explain the situation in-house. That meant, assuming the public announcement was made in September, that the in-house announcement would have to be made at the beginning of August. It would consist of notifying everyone of Miya-san's retirement and Ghibli's restructuring.

To tell the truth, running Ghibli was far too expensive. The production costs for *The Wind Rises* alone were an astronomical 5 billion yen. And if the studio's chief moneymaker retired, it would be extremely difficult to maintain the company's viability.

We therefore had no choice but to think about disbanding the staff after every film and reassembling it for each new one. Naturally, this would be done only after consulting with President Hoshino and others.

Since Miya-san customarily spent the month of August at a mountain retreat, preparations for the in-house meeting were made in his absence. But then, just before the meeting Miya-san suddenly said, "I want to take part in the meeting and bring this chapter in my life to a close."

The meeting consisted of the principal members of the various divisions, about thirty people in all. Everyone was waiting breathlessly for what Miya-san would say, but he couldn't bring himself to broach the subject. Since he is usually a talkative person, tension was high in the room. When he finally spoke, he simply said, "I can't do it anymore." He seemed to be saying that, having realized that he couldn't carry on as usual, he had no choice but to give up filmmaking. Having said that, he then clamped his mouth shut, as if he had nothing more to say. Less than three minutes had passed since he started speaking.

## The Press Conference

The press conference to announce Miya-san's retirement took place on September 6. Just before that date he said to me, "Suzuki-san, is a press conference really necessary?" What in the world is he saying, I thought. It had been his idea to have a press conference. "I'll still be doing some work," he went on. "I'll still be doing what I want to do. I just won't be doing feature films." This was a little different from his original idea. [Laughs] On September 5, the day before the conference, he showed up and handed me a sheet of paper. It was his "official retirement statement." The first line read, "I want to work for at least ten more years." How he must have agonized over this!

At the press conference Miya-san spoke of everything he had thought or felt from the past to the present. He tried his best to answer the questions posed by the journalists. Most memorable of all—though I had heard it before—was what he said about how hard it was to be a director, which I knew all too well myself. Once, just after finishing *Nausicaä*, he said, "I don't want to direct ever again. I don't want to lose any more friends." And furthermore: "I just wanted to draw, to be an animator. That was my true calling in life. Drawing a good shot really made me happy." He was speaking from the heart, I believe.

While Miya-san was delivering his retirement speech, I was sitting at his side. Hearing his remarks, I couldn't help but feel a certain sense of relief. When I was asked my feelings about Miya-san's retirement, I could honestly say they consisted of appreciation for his hard work in addition to personal relief. They were a mixture of both. In making *The Wind Rises* Miya-san had summoned every ounce of strength at his command. But compared to his younger days, he wasn't as energetic as he used to be. It was a matter of technical prowess. Having worked with him over many a year, I could feel the difference. He had definitely reached, I felt, a certain limit to his abilities. I wanted to say, from the bottom of my heart, "I'm grateful for all your hard work over the years." As for myself, I had engaged in all kinds of projects in the last thirty years, but now, thinking that the end might be near, I felt a sense of liberation.

When the press conference came to an end, we reached out, very naturally and without either taking the initiative, and shook hands. Just think, shaking hands with Miya-san! It was the first time this had happened in thirty years. I have to admit that I was dumbstruck.

## Seiichiro Ujiie's Dream: *The Tale of The Princess Kaguya*

On November 23, a little more than two months after Miya-san's retirement press conference, Takahata's *The Tale of The Princess Kaguya* was released. It was his first work in fourteen years. This film would never have seen the light of day without the support of Seiichiro Ujiie, then chairman of Nippon Television Network Corporation and a great fan of Takahata's work. He declared that he wanted to see something new by Takahata and pledged to provide financial and other support to realize that end. He carried out his promise, which is the reason his name appears prominently in the credits as Executive Producer. Unfortunately, he passed away in 2011 and never saw the final film.

Before talking about the film itself, I would like to say a few words about Ujiie-san. One of the conditions for producing a blockbuster film, I believe, is the presence of a patron. It is only when there is a supportive patron who understands the director and his work that an ambitious film can be undertaken. In the past, that person had been President Tokuma. After Tokuma's passing, Ujiie-san inherited and expanded on that role. In his book *Showa to iu jidai o ikite* (My Life in the Showa Period; 2012), he entreats Takahata: "Please produce good movies that will last." Speaking as the chairman of Nippon TV, he plainly said in the first chapter of his book, "Jiburi to watashi" (Ghibli and Me), that he would take responsibility for his words.

I still have fond memories of Ujiie-san. His support was instrumental in founding the Ghibli Museum, Mitaka, and after its completion he served as chairman of The Tokuma Memorial Cultural Foundation for Animation, which was in charge of the museum's management. It was then that I began to see him on a periodic basis. Since the chairman was equivalent to the president of a company, I would go every month to report on recent activities. Being a busy man, he would usually allot time for a thirty-minute meeting, but when I went, the meeting would last at least an hour, sometimes two. When I got ready to leave, he would get miffed and say, "What, leaving already?" Strangely enough, we seemed to hit it off, to be somehow compatible.

I have an interesting story about the time he was appointed director of the Museum of Contemporary Art Tokyo. I got a call from him one day, and he asked, "Suzu-chan, do you know the Museum of Contemporary Art Tokyo?"

"No," I said. "I've never heard of it."

"Just as I expected. It's located in Kiba. Anyway, I'm going to be appointed its director. I haven't told anyone else yet. Just you."

As I was puzzling over why he had called me, he said, "I want your help."

"I'll help out as long as you are still breathing," I told him.

"Okay, that's good. As long as I am still breathing then; we have a deal." There was something particularly engaging about his manner.

Thanks to this connection, a number of Ghibli-related exhibitions were held at the museum. They included *Sutajio Jiburi rittai-zokeibutsu-ten* (Studio Ghibli: Architecture in Animation), *Kyutai kansetsu ningyo-ten* (Dolls of Innocence), *Nihon manga-eiga no zenbo* (Japanese Animated Films: A Complete View from their Birth to "Spirited Away" and Beyond), *"Hauru no ugoku shiro" daisakasu-ten* (The circus exhibition of the [sic] "Howl's Moving Castle"), *Dizuni ato-ten* (The Art of Disney), *Jiburi no e-shokunin: Oga Kazuo-ten* (Kazuo Oga Exhibition), *Sutajio Jiburi*

August 22, 2009, Arezzo, Italy. At Ujiie's suggestion, Suzuki, Miyazaki, Takahata, and Ujiie made a trip to Europe. Here, in Suzuki's photograph, Miyazaki is seen on the left, Takahata in the middle, and Ujiie on the right.

*reiauto-ten* (Studio Ghibli Layout Designs: Understanding the Secrets of Takahata/Miyazaki Animation), *Meari Burea-ten* (The Colors of Mary Blair), and *Karigurashi no Arietti x Taneda Yohei-ten* (Karigurashi no Arrietty & Yohei Taneda: Fusing Fantasy with Reality). Many people came to see these exhibitions, and Ujiie-san was very thankful for my assistance.

As I mentioned above, Ujiie's dream was to see the completion of Takahata's *Tale of The Princess Kaguya*. Just before passing away, he read the screenplay and looked through the half-completed storyboards. His impression of the work was very typical of him: "Princess Kaguya is the type of girl who gets what she wants. I like that kind of girl." When I passed that along to Takahata—verbatim—he broke out into a broad smile, completely satisfied. Takahata had long said that he wanted to do "Princess Kaguya" as a modern story.

## *The Tale of The Princess Kaguya* Encounters Strong Headwinds

From acceptance of the project to its completion, *Princess Kaguya* consumed something like eight years. The producer, Yoshiaki Nishimura, was twenty-six at the time preparations got underway. He is now thirty-six, no longer one of Ghibli's youngsters but a core member.

Since Takahata is a stickler for detail and very persistent, it was decided from the beginning to use a small number of outsourced staff and not skimp on time. Takahata wanted it that way, and I had my own reasons. *The Wind Rises* would be produced solely by Ghibli staff on the one hand, and *Princess Kaguya* would be made entirely by outsourced staff on the other. Recruiting the right people for a one-off project was the system employed by Ghibli in its early days. I wanted to treat this project as an experiment and see what could be accomplished, including the problems of staff formation and money matters. That's why, when Nishimura asked to use Ghibli staff for the film, I put a damper on the idea. "Outsource it," I told him.

Still, the project was progressing at a snail's pace. Nishimura informed me, "Storyboard production is inching along at the rate of two minutes a month. Since the start of the project, it's taken five years to do thirty minutes." Takahata's original screenplay was an extraordinarily long three and a half hours, and only after considerable cutting was it brought down to two and half hours (the finished product was two hours and seventeen minutes long). At this pace, the movie would reach completion around 2020. Given that we were dealing with Takahata, even that wasn't certain. So I put the question to Nishimura: "Which is more important—the film or Takahata?" It's true that a project that seems endless has a certain attraction. It is sort of fun working on something like that. But what did Nishimura think; that was the important point. He said, "It's the film that's important. Somehow I want to see it finished." I replied, "That means Takahata has to be sacked." By that time, the storyboards had been finished, and everyone could pitch in and get it done, even without Takahata. Nishimura and I had reached that point in our discussions of the problem. Takahata had always said that if he were fired by the producer, he would have to accept it, so I thought if it came to that, Takahata would acquiesce. In the end, Takahata agreed to increase the number of staff and pick up the pace. Given Takahata's personality, this was quite a concession.

In the magazine *Switch* (December, 2013), when speaking with Nobuo Kawakami, Nishimura described the scene when *Princess Kaguya* was finally finished.

> *When the final touches had been put on the film, Takahata turned in my direction and said, "Is that it? If I give the word, is that it?" When I said, "Yes, that's it," he said, "I wanted to do more...." Then he went on for an interminable two or three hours making what seemed to be unnecessary changes. He didn't want the film to be finished.*

## The Obsession with Line and Negative Space

Everyone who has seen *Princess Kaguya* is in agreement about one thing: the drawings are exquisitely rendered. This applies particularly to line and the way of expressing negative space (*yohaku*). Takahata was especially concerned with line: its lightness or darkness, its thickness, the beginning and ending of individual strokes of the brush. The in-between animators practically had to trace the lines of the drawings done by the key animators. This process verged on madness, and it was terribly time-consuming. It might take twice as long to finish, or three or four or five times as long. I will not go into technical detail here, but it is fair to say that this approach is suited only to short pieces. There is no one in the world who would attempt to do this with a feature film. That's why I told Takahata at the beginning: "Why don't you try this on a short piece"? But Takahata was too ambitious for his own good; he wasn't interested in making an experimental movie. He wanted to do a feature entertainment film. He wanted it be seen by a wide audience.

The person who made all this possible was Osamu Tanabe. Nishimura said of him, "Just as Miyazaki enters into his characters and infuses them with emotion, Tanabe infuses his work with sensuous feeling." Tanabe is listed in the film's credits as being responsible for character design and directing animator. In fact, he enabled Takahata to achieve his aims. A huge contribution was also made by Kazuo Oga, the art director. In the press release, Nishimura wrote:

> *No matter how absurd the schedule became, Osamu Tanabe and Kazuo Oga were there to put their genius to work and ensure that we did not swerve from the project's original intent. Finally we reached what Mr. Takahata calls that "point of arrival," "the realization of a kind of dream."*

In this respect Takahata is quite different from Miya-san. The nuances of *Princess Kaguya* emerge from its delicate expressiveness, but this special flavor would certainly disappear if the conventional line work of in-between drawing was employed. For his part, Miya-san believed it was his duty to adhere to the conventions of mass entertainment, and felt that nuanced lines were going too far. He would usually decide on a certain type of line and stick to it. Of course, Miya-san himself would have preferred a more nuanced treatment, like the Canadian Frédéric Back, who did all the drawings for his films with his own hand. However, Miya-san considered that to be outside the realm of popular entertainment.

## Frédéric Back and John Lasseter

The above-mentioned master filmmaker Frédéric Back won two Academy Awards for Animated Short Film with *Crac* (1981) and *L'homme qui plantait des arbres* (The Man Who Planted Trees; 1987). Takahata revered him as a mentor for "both his films and his way of life," and keenly wanted to show him the finished *Princess Kaguya*. In December 2013 we visited Canada and the United States. The purported reason for the trip was the North American promotion of *Princess Kaguya*, but Takahata's real goal was to visit Montreal and show Back his film.

At the time, Back was struggling with cancer, and his condition was critical. But since it was Takahata who was asking, he welcomed our visit and viewed the whole film. He said, "It's absolutely beautiful. The usage of negative space [*yohaku*] is particularly remarkable." I imagine that this is exactly what Takahata had hoped to hear. One week after we returned to Japan, on December 24, Back drew his last breath at his home in Canada. He was eighty-nine.

So how did the North American promotion pan out—which was, after all, the ostensible purpose of the trip? We showed the film to Pixar's John Lasseter, who had actually already seen part of it before it was finished. When Lasseter came to Japan to see *The Wind Rises*, it was decided to make use of the opportunity and have him drop by the *Princess Kaguya* studio. Seeing the film, he became excited beyond belief.... The reason was that, besides making 3D animations, he was also immensely interested in hand-drawn 2D movies and was actively involved in seeing that they didn't disappear from the American scene. He was astounded at the quality of expression and wanted to know how it had been achieved. Until the very last minute he bombarded Takahata with questions. But when we took the finished film to the United States, he said unequivocally that it was not a film for the mass market. "The technical expression has been an inspiration. But, in the end, it is art. So in the United States it would be best to release it in art-house type theaters." I myself was of the same opinion, so after that we didn't pursue the matter any further.

### How *The Wind Rises* Was Received

When a new film is released, I always estimate the crowd we might expect, and I am not often wrong. With *Princess Kaguya*, however, I wasn't sure at all. In terms of box office, the results were pretty severe. It grossed 2.5 billion yen. While there were people who found the film immensely interesting, overall it didn't show signs of reaching out to a wider audience. One problem, to my mind, was that it was too long for mass appeal. On the other hand, it is true that the film began to evince unexpected movement not long after its release: the audience began to grow. I think this is connected to the nature of the film. People interested in artistic expression were really impressed. In any case, Takahata had expressed his all in the film, and that was enough, I thought. I wasn't at all shocked by the box office results.

What did shock me was something else entirely. It was the way young people reacted to the ending: "What the...? Is she returning to the moon?" This was mentioned by more than a few younger viewers.

In other words, they were just following the story; they weren't interested in the artistic expression. As for myself, I have seen a lot of films in my time, and while I may retain only a vague memory of the story, certain scenes remain fixed indelibly in my mind. What impressed me was their means of expression. I wonder that younger viewers don't watch movies in this way. What they look for in a movie is diametrically different. That's what I found shocking. Nowadays, interest in artistic technique has flown out the window; readers are concerned merely with the complications of plot. This is the age we now live in, I thought to myself anew.

### Miya-san's and Takahata's Films

In making *The Wind Rises* and *Princess Kaguya*, Miya-san and Takahata each gave it their best shot. I think they both must have felt a certain sense of satisfaction, a feeling of accomplishment, in finishing the films. Miya-san, as usual, kept doing drawings himself, giving instructions to the key animators, and making amendments. He had a hand in tens of thousands of drawings. Takahata, for his part, worked every day until two o'clock in the morning during the last month of production. He was already seventy-eight years old, mind you. I did my best to keep up with them, but I was dead tired at the end.

I devoted myself to seeing that they could create what their hearts desired. I got the necessary funds, and I opened up a schedule for their work. Up until then I had been much in their debt, but now I felt that I had returned some of what I owed them. I don't want to talk about money, but the two films together cost an unprecedented 10 billion yen. Hearing of this, the various companies involved in the project were stunned. They asked me, "How are you ever going to get it all back?"

What I wanted to say in response was: Oh, just forget about all that! Miya-san and Takahata have put their hearts and souls into these two works. Remember how much you have benefited from their films in the past.

In hindsight I can't help thinking that all of the films Miya-san and Takahata have made for Ghibli, not just these two, are best seen by boys and girls who are just reaching adulthood. Some people say that *The Wind Rises* is an adult movie, but I think that is absolute bull. The movie has a hero and a sustaining heroine.... It gains meaning only when watched by younger people. In his retirement speech Miya-san had this to say:

> *I entered this world under the influence of the many children's books I had read. At the time I considered it the crux of my work to pass on to young people the idea that "life is worth living." That remains unchanged today.*

When the question arises as to why Ghibli has managed to capture the hearts of people around the world, many say that it is due to the films' wonderful themes. But I disagree. I think it is expression, the power of artistic expression. Take *My Neighbor Totoro,* for example. There is the scene where Mei gets on Totoro's belly and is leaping about. She is so obviously enjoying herself. To give expression to a scene like this with only a pencil—this is the power and appeal of animation. How many other animators are capable of this kind of expression? None, I think. Here we see Miya-san's greatness. As Takahata said, hitting the nail right on the head, "Miya-san's works appeal to the senses."

## The Academy Awards Ceremony

As for how Ghibli's films were received abroad, I have one interesting story concerning the Academy Awards ceremonies held in March 2014. Previously, when *Spirited Away* received an award, no one from Ghibli had attended the ceremony. My going this time, for *The Wind*

*Rises*, would be a first. Aside from the ceremony itself, what I found particularly interesting was the panel discussion held two days before. The directors and producers of the animated feature films that had been nominated were all in attendance. Near the end we were asked to name one animated feature of particular note among all those we had seen. To my amazement, everyone mentioned a Miyazaki film. There was even one person who, uttering the words *Spirited Away*, broke down in tears. That shows the extent to which Miya-san is revered. He is a virtual god. I was dumbfounded.

The eventual winner of the Oscar was Disney's *Frozen*, directed by Chris Buck and Jennifer Lee, who had both named a Miyazaki film at the panel discussion. They were terribly conscious of my presence. The evening before the awards, Pixar's John Lasseter, *Frozen*'s executive producer, held a joint party for Ghibli and Disney, but the two directors didn't come over to chat with me, and they kept their eyes averted. [Laughs] They were awfully nervous. In the end, when they won the Oscar, they were moved to tears.

To return to the earlier panel discussion, there was one thing that gave me pause. The moderator asked me, "Is it true that you discouraged Miyazaki from doing a movie he was planning to produce and encouraged him to make *The Wind Rises* instead?" I said that was true and explained the background. At this time the discussion didn't go any further than that, but later I was told that American producers these days adhere to what has been successful in the past and don't produce any new ideas, that *The Wind Rises* was a risky venture as entertainment, and that it would have been unthinkable in the United States for a producer to go against the wishes of a director and support the undertaking of a film like *The Wind Rises*. Et cetera, et cetera. I was a bit startled at these pronouncements, but later came to see some truth in them. The general trend in the United States does seem to lean toward safe choices and remakes. That may not be far off the mark, I thought.

## The Role of a Realist

In the words of one individual, Miya-san is an entertainer and Takahata an artist. This may be true, but more important than that is the fact that they are both a type of idealist. Further, the fact that I have been able to work with them for such a long time is due to my being a realist, I think. That I have always handled problems in a coolheaded, practical manner accounts for our long-lived relationship. Takahata once told me, "Of all the people, I have met in my life, you are the most coolheaded."

To tell the truth, I like movies made for adults, like Yasujiro Ozu's *Tokyo monogatari* (Tokyo Story). [Laughs] I actually don't get action-adventure films, which may explain why I'm able to stay focused. You could even say that since this was not a world that I entered through personal infatuation, I was able to treat the work as work and cut to the core. In fact, it is not a good thing for the producer to get too fired up. He loses sight of what is in front of his eyes. Of course, just being levelheaded doesn't guarantee success, but fundamentally it is best to stay calm and collected.

Perhaps because I am a realist I don't identify with the story heart and soul, but treat it as an object. For example, with the 124-minute *Spirited Away* I calculated from the storyboards how long each character appeared in the story. It didn't matter how important the scene was—I just counted how many minutes the characters appeared. Broken down by character, Chihiro was at the top of the list, with No Face next. While this was a purely mechanical process, I believe it reflected the director's deeper thinking. As a result, I shifted the film's advertising to focus on Chihiro and No Face. As mentioned earlier in chapter 4, I was a little nonplussed when Miya-san suddenly asked me about this. [Laughs] Further, I also counted the number of lines each character spoke. For *Only Yesterday* I also did the following. When the screenplay was finally finished, I read through it with a staff member, placing a clock at my side. One of a producer's biggest worries is production costs, which are determined by the length of the film. I wrote down the number of seconds for individual lines in the scenario and showed the result to Takahata. I told him that this was the film's current length and asked him to reduce it by so many minutes. Takahata responded, "So that's what you've been up to! In all my years working on animation, you're the first one to do anything like this." I don't know if that's what did the trick, but the film did get shorter.

## The Problems Confronting Ghibli

It is now 2014, almost thirty years since the establishment of Ghibli in 1985. The studio is facing a major turning point. At the beginning, staff were assembled for the making of each film and then disbanded when the film was finished. Then, at Miya-san's suggestion, a studio was built to serve as a production center, and staff were employed on a permanent basis. Some twenty years have passed since then, and I think this system has proven successful. A program for training new staff was also established, and it has produced many excellent animators over the years. Many of them are now active elsewhere in the animation world, and I can't help thinking that their experience at Ghibli has proven to be of considerable value. This has not so much to do with Studio Ghibli as a company, but with the role these animators have played in raising the overall level of Japanese animation. This has been possible in large part because of the existence of Hayao Miyazaki. Unfortunately, it is an undeniable fact that the cost of maintaining this system has risen from one year to the next. There are definite limits to self-subsistence.

In passing, I might mention that I was against the idea of resolving this problem by expanding related businesses. We had any number of proposals for selling related goods such as character toys, but if we took this route, it would inevitably develop into a business in its own right. Ghibli had been founded to make films, on the model of a small neighborhood factory manned by master craftsmen. If the company suddenly transformed itself into a producer of character goods, who could tell why it had been established in the first place? This is precisely why we have scrupulously kept the sales of related goods within certain set boundaries.

After reviewing and assessing the system previously employed, we had to change the way films were produced. The litmus test for this new venture would be *Omoide no Mani* (When Marnie Was There), released in the summer of 2014.

## A New Start with *When Marnie Was There*

In January 2012, when we were still working on *The Wind Rises*, Hiromasa Yonebayashi (that is, Maro) came to me and said, "I want to direct another film." When I asked him why, he told me, "There is still something I want to accomplish as a director." I immediately gave him a copy of Joan G. Robinson's novel *When Marnie Was There* (Japanese translation published in Iwanami's Shonen Bunko).

*Marnie* had been on my mind for some time, and there were three reasons I thought that Maro would be a suitable director. The first was that the story was centered around two girls. I imagined that Maro had been fond of drawing girl characters since he was in his teens. Just as Miya-san enjoyed drawing fighter planes, Maro probably had a steadfast liking for drawing girls. I was certain that he would enjoy differentiating the two characters. Second, I had the feeling that the resultant film would be different from what Miya-san might produce. Most likely, Miya-san couldn't make a movie like *Marnie*. *Marnie* would be deeper and more nuanced than anything Ghibli had previously produced. Maro was clearly more sensitive than Miya-san, and he was younger. I instinctively felt that his film would have an appeal that differed from Miya-san's fantasy films. The third reason was that there were no male characters. In most stories, whether the protagonist is male or female, the usual pattern is for a person of the opposite sex to be instrumental in resolving the protagonist's predicament. In the case of *Marnie*, however, the issue is resolved without any male characters. I thought this very modern.

Even before Maro approached me about directing a film, something had been preying on my mind. Miya-san had announced his retirement, and Takahata had reached a certain critical age in his life. The question was: should we leave a gap before the next film or should we continue to produce without a break? After giving the matter a good deal of thought, I reached the conclusion that it would be best to continue without a break. When it became apparent that the two directors had reached an end to their careers, it was precisely then, I thought, that a new, hopeful light for the future should be introduced. That's when Maro showed up. "Okay," I thought, "let's do it."

At the same time I had another idea: I would change my present role. Nishimura had done a great job on *Princess Kaguya*, so I would have him produce *Marnie*, and I would become general manager. A general manager marshals the necessary forces, constructs the overall framework, and then leaves the rest to the staff. That much I would do, leaving the rest to Maro and Nishimura.

## Assembling the Best Possible Staff

First of all, I worked out the general plan and decided the direction of the scenario. Keiko Niwa would write the script. I brought Masashi Ando and Yohei Taneda on board as core members of the team. After that, I left the rest to on-site staff under the direction of Nishimura.

Ando would be supervising the animation. He had played a big role in *Princess Mononoke* and *Spirited Away*, but had subsequently left Ghibli to work elsewhere. He had reemerged to participate in *Princess Kaguya*, and said he wanted to take part in a film by Takahata.

I asked him if he would lend Maro a helping hand in making *Marnie*. In fact, he was Maro's senior and hoped to play a larger part in film direction. After reading the novel and looking over the scenario, he proposed some ideas on how the animation might be produced so that it would be more faithful to the original. When I asked Maro what he thought about these ideas, he had no objections. In fact, he very much wanted Ando to take part in the creation of *Marnie* and expressly said he wanted his help. In the end, the final screenplay was a collaborative effort by Niwa, Ando, and Maro.

The next issue was art direction, which brings us to Yohei Taneda. He was at the top of his class in production design for Japanese movies. I had a past connection with him and was familiar with his work, so I recommended him to Maro. Maro said he would be delighted to have him. True, Taneda had no experience in animation, but he was superb at what he did. When I brought the subject up, he thankfully accepted. So animation would be handled by Ando, and background art by Taneda. With the participation of these two, a formidable core was established.

In addition to this, a fortuitous cycle of events evolved. As mentioned earlier, when Nishimura was working on *Princess Kaguya*, the policy was to outsource everything, and as a result he came into contact with many capable animators. These animators now joined the team. Furthermore, the main animators who had been slated for *Neon Genesis Evangelion*, the production of which was delayed for various reasons, now came over to *Marnie*. The result was the formation of the greatest imaginable contingent of animators in present-day Japan.

## The Key to Advertising: The Catchphrase

With Nishimura in control of on-site staff, production was proceeding apace, and the time to start advertising was approaching. Advertising is one of a producer's most important jobs, and initially I told

Nishimura that he should handle it. His response was that he didn't have a good grasp of advertising, and he wanted me to do it for him just one more time. Appealed to in this way, I had no choice but to settle down to work and come up with some good ideas.

Advertising starts with the catchphrase, an approach which may be unique to Ghibli. Advertising copy, or "catch copy," will have its own impact in one way or another, but it is the catchphrase that determines the direction of the advertising and gives it concrete form. The catchphrase must encapsulate the core appeal of the film, its very essence.

This fact was brought home to me with *Princess Mononoke*. When I decided on the catchphrase "Live" for *Princess Mononoke*, there was a great deal of adverse commentary from professionals in the field, but I stuck to my guns. In effect, this was one of the factors that determined the direction that advertising would take in making the film a success. The catchphrase for *Spirited Away* was "Reawaken the will to live." Both of these catchphrases have a deep connection with human life. It was by giving prominence to keywords like this that the power to attract viewers was generated.

A simple illustration of this approach is *The Cat Returns*. The poster for this film shows the heroine lying in a field of grass. The copy reads: "The country of cats. A place to go for those who don't have the time to live their own lives. What's wrong with becoming a cat?" What was important here was to catch the mood of the day. After all, we live in stressful times. As it turned out, the film grossed 6.4 billion yen. With ordinary advertising, the most you could expect would be 1 or 2 billion—at least that's what one person familiar with the industry told me. Advertising is that powerful, and at its core is the catchphrase.

So what should be done with *Marnie*? A lot of ideas were presented, but there was no consensus. Nothing seemed exactly right. When thinking about advertising copy, two parts of the brain must be called into play. One part is structural and logical, the other instinctive and intuitive. When asking everyone what they thought, what suddenly popped into my head was "Just know that I love you." This happened when we had run out of time, when we were clinging to the edge of a cliff by our fingernails. Maybe we live in times when people are searching for someone they can say these words to, or someone who will say, "Just know that I love you." These words don't depend on logic for their power; they are simple and fresh. Interestingly, *daisuki*, translated as "love" in the above, can be written in two ways in Japanese: 大すき and 大好き. The former, which was used in the advertising copy, is much more familiar and friendly. The power of words is a mysterious thing.

There was unanimous agreement on this catchphrase, and everyone immediately set to work. Even the content of the trailer, which had yet to be started, would be influenced. I hoped that this would be interpreted as signaling a fresh start for Ghibli.

## Thirty Years Brings One Stage to an End

I have always thought, and have publicly said, that thirty years would mark one stage in my working life. Now it's time for the next step. There are still many things I want to do, but I don't intend to aim for some remotely distant goal. I have always preferred to work steadily away at what is right in front of me. In *Minna no negai* (Everyone's Wish), published by the Japanese Association for the Study of Issues Facing People with Disabilities (October 2013), I said the following:

> *I believe that there are two ways of living. One is to set up a distant goal and work steadily toward achieving it. This is not something easily done, however, and I have never set such goals for myself. The other way is to work steadily at what is immediately in front of you and thereby discover what you are most suited to do. This, in my mind, is what it means to "live."*
>
> *In doing this, you will undoubtedly meet with adversity, but in*

> *fact adversity is something you should enjoy. The trick is to think of it as happening to someone else. By looking at the problems confronting you in an objective manner, you can sometimes find a solution.*

This is still my basic stance in life, to chip steadily away at immediate problems. Basically, I have taken a passive approach, dealing with problems as they come up and believing that the future will take care of itself. This was true of the past and remains true today.

But having come this far in life, I can't help noticing certain things. In order to create successful movies, I have been an observer of the movements of society, and it seems to me that we have entered an age in which people no longer want to think—a very disturbing development. I generally don't like speaking out about matters aside from filmmaking, but the fact that I have spoken out about Article 9 of the Japanese constitution, as well as the issue of nuclear power, is an indication of my sense of crisis. Every day new things crop up that I should speak out on—now or never—given the urgent times we live in.

I would like to take the time to think seriously about what filmmaking means. After all, movies are a mirror of the times. It is also true that movies, whether on TV or in theaters, are facing incomparably tougher times in their ability to attract viewers. As a producer, what should I do in the present situation? It is still unclear to me, but I plan to continue to think about it in the present progressive tense. How will it turn out? The future lies before me.

# Afterword to the Original Japanese Edition (2008): How Films Result from Casual Conversation

How did this book come about?

According to my records, it was on December 16, 2005, almost two and a half years ago, when I first met Kazuo Inoue, the head of sales at the publisher Iwanami Shoten. We had been discussing a tie-in for *Tales from Earthsea* when Inoue suddenly said, “Why don’t you publish a book with us?”

My immediate response was that this was out of the question, but still, there was something about Inoue that intrigued me. First of all, he had formerly been an editor, and had handled the bestseller *Daiojo* (A Peaceful Passing; 1994) by the multitalented essayist Rokusuke Ei. As someone who had worked in the same field, I couldn’t entirely turn a deaf ear to what he had to say. Given my background, I was still interested in the publishing world and the latest bestsellers.

As we were talking, there was one thing that I instantly realized. He was the type of person who grasped the big picture and didn’t worry about trivial details. He had trained himself to see things from a broad perspective. In the best meaning of the word he was easygoing, but he somehow combined this with exactness. He had a certain charm about him and was always attentive to the person he was talking to. He possessed delicacy. In fact, he was a model editor. Moreover, I couldn’t help noticing that he and I were the same age.

As to why he wanted to publish a book by me, he was brutally frank, and laughingly said, “I have no interest in Miyazaki or Takahata, but I am interested in you. Most people can't hope to become a genius like Miyazaki or Takahata, but they can learn something from you."

How cheeky can you get, I thought—how downright rude! But looking back, I realized that this was the attitude I often took when meeting someone for the first time. In any case, this is how Inoue became indelibly etched in my mind.

Not long afterward, Iwanami would publish successive books by Takahata and Miyazaki: respectively, *Manga eiga no kokorozashi* (The Aspirations of Manga Films) and *Burakkamu no bakugeki-ki* (Blackham's Wimpy). By publishing books by two directors in whom he had no interest, Inoue signified that he had given up publishing a book by me. "Well, that's the end of that," I thought to myself, chuckling. I had bested Inoue.

After that, I didn't hear again from Inoue. Then one day, to celebrate the publication of *The Aspirations of Manga Films*, Takahata, Yukari Tai (of Ghibli's publishing department), and I were invited to dinner at a Chinese restaurant near the Iwanami offices. As we were leaving the restaurant, Inoue suddenly approached and whispered in my ear, "Now it's your turn."

I was caught completely off guard. After all, as I said earlier, I thought that the book idea had been settled. Inoue hadn't forgotten, though. I wasn't sure how to respond, but in the end we agreed to meet again and discuss the matter.

Not long after this, I clearly remember Takahata coming to me and saying, "Inoue had you in mind all along."

That was the summer of 2007, which is when the book got started.

Inoue's proposal went as follows. The book would be dictated, and the overall tone would reflect that format. The interviewer would be Inoue himself; most surprising of all, he said he would also make the manuscript draft. Frankly, I had my doubts about the head of sales becoming this involved in the project. He said, "I'll do all this over the holidays." In the end I had to bow to his intense energy. The editor in charge of the book, Yoshiko Furukawa, would also be there. She would record the interviews in writing and put the manuscript in order. Ghibli's Yukari Tai, who had been a colleague of mine at *Animage*, would also take part.

My assistant, Nobuko Shiraki, collected the writings and magazine interviews I had published over the years and handed them over to Inoue.

The interviews for the book took place one after another without a hitch, and everything seemed to be going smoothly. But somewhere along the line I began to feel ill at ease. I had once been an editor and was now a producer. My job was to place people on a cutting board and chop them up for ingredients, so to speak. To have the positions reversed was proving to be very stressful.

Just at that moment, an excellent opportunity arose for relieving built-up tension. In October, as part of the Japan International Contents Festival, which was sponsored by the Ministry of Economy, Trade and Industry, there was an event called the Dramatic Three-hour Show, and they wanted me to take part. I was told that I could make use of three hours to do whatever I wanted. Ordinarily I would have turned down the offer, but certain reasons made this difficult. One was that the person who raised the subject was Yutaka Shigenobu of TV Man Union, to whom I was indebted for past favors. In addition, according to Shigenobu, I had been recommended by Nippon TV's Seiichiro Ujiie.

I was struggling with the problem of what I could do when an idea popped into my head: What if I conducted one of the interviews for the forthcoming book on the three-hour show? I would have Inoue appear on the program, and in the process I would kill four birds with one stone. I would be fulfilling my duty to the Contents Festival, completing one of the interviews, placing Inoue on a cutting board, and—best of all—relieving some of my stress.

That was my devious plan, but I had forgotten that Inoue is the type of person who turns every situation to his advantage. He came fully prepared, having tidied up and organized our most recent interviews. I had made no preparations myself and hadn't even been told what topics Inoue as interviewer would bring up. The outcome was as you might expect: I was placed once more on the chopping block.

After the show was over, Shigenobu hosted a little party, which is where I heard something rather interesting from Inoue. He said, "The English word *editor* is often translated as *henshu-sha*, but I think that is a mistake. In the West, *editor* literally means someone who edits the text, but in Japan that is not usually the case."

This left an impression on my mind, and I could picture an image of the Japanese editor as described by Inoue. Typically, what most Japanese editors do for authors is to engage them in casual conversation. It is from these conversations that the final work is born. This is the obverse of the Western editor's way of working, which begins with a discussion of the theme. It is the archetypical Japanese approach, and a source of pride. I even deluded myself into thinking that Inoue was of the same mind. If that were the case, then I could see Inoue's motivation for producing the present book.

I recall him saying, "I remember you calling yourself an editorial-type producer, which aroused my interest." I was in complete agreement with this description.

The job of a producer has an entirely different meaning in Japan and the West. In the West, films are often made with the producer taking the lead. The director is nothing more than an employee hired by the producer. In Japan, on the other hand, the producer helps plan the film through casual discussion with the director, who is the central figure.

As if to back up this thought, when I appeared on NHK's *The Ways of Professionals* (a.k.a. *The Professionals*), Miya-san contributed this comment: "He keeps your nose to the grindstone while pretending not to. He fires you up while pretending not to."

In the end I decided to leave everything in Inoue's hands. The editor Yoshiko Furukawa thought up the title of the book.

P.S.
There is an individual at Ghibli named Shinsuke Nonaka. He is the type who relies on recorded fact rather than memory. I had him take a look at the manuscript. One after another, errors of memory came tumbling out. The chronology appended to this book is also his work.

Toshio Suzuki
June 2008

## Afterword to the Revised Japanese Edition (2014): A Word about Flowers

I would like to say something about flowers. I am fond of moth orchids (*Phalaenopsis*). Why should that be? Because my mother liked them. That's the only reason I can think of.

I have a grandson. He was named Rando (Orchid Dignity). That was the first time I heard that my daughter liked orchids. She wanted her son to grow up to be a young man who was strong like an orchid. So it seems that four generations of our family have been orchid lovers.

When I received the Minister of Education, Culture, Sports, Science and Technology's Art Encouragement Prize, masses of orchids were sent by friends and colleagues in congratulations. As a result, my room was awash with flowers. My mother kept saying, "Oh, how pretty!" and my daughter took photos of Rando surrounded by the orchids. Rando was tremendously pleased.

My mother turned ninety-one this spring, my daughter thirty-eight; Rando is two years old. I myself am sixty-five. Four generations are living under the same roof.

Incidentally, when I was awarded the Art Encouragement Prize, I was honored to receive many words of congratulations from various quarters. It was apparently quite extraordinary for a producer to be the recipient of this prize. In filmmaking, the prize had previously been awarded to directors and on-site staff for their artistic creativity.

When I first got the call about the prize, I thought it was just another award for Miya-san and didn't really pay much attention. He himself had already gone into retirement, of course. When it hit me that this wasn't the case, my initial reaction was, "Oh, what am I going to do about this?"

Just before that, there had been some misinformed reports speculating about my imminent retirement, and this had been a terrible nuisance. I got heaps of messages saying, "Congratulations on your retirement and kudos for your long career," and queries from abroad about the matter. They all seemed intent on forcing me into retirement. So my emotions were mixed about the prize, feeling that it was a new attempt at encouraging me to retire. You may think it is a little late to be mentioning this now, but the work of a producer takes place behind the scenes, and his creative contributions are virtually nil. Even so, in the course of events producers are sometimes criticized for pushing themselves too far to the front. If I waffled about the prize now, though, I would be stepping on the toes of numerous kind people. Such thoughts instantly occurred to me as I was talking on the phone, and so I decided to accept the prize without a fuss.

Orchids in vases began to arrive at the studio, coming to the notice of Miya-san. As if to forestall any reservations on my part, he told me plainly, "Are you getting a prize or something? You should definitely accept it."

Coming from a man who was always thinking of reasons for not accepting prizes, this made me happier than anything else.

When I was asked to add something to the 2008 afterword to this book, I wasn't quite sure what to do. I couldn't think of anything to write. We had just entered the year 2014 and were continuing with the interviews for this book, together with Kazuo Inoue and the editor in charge, Yoshiko Furukawa, who was faithfully doing the transcribing as before. Ghibli's Yukari Tai was also there. The deadline for the interviews and the revised edition of the book was drawing near. Almost at the same time, the cutoff date for the monthly series appearing in the *Chunichi* newspaper (to be published on March 27, 2014) was also fast approaching. I wrote that piece first. When I showed it to Furukawa, she suggested that I use it as-is for the new afterword. Inoue remarked that it accurately reflected my present state of mind. Tai was in complete agreement. I hadn't shown them the piece with anything like that in mind, but reading it from their perspective, I thought they might be right. Frankly it was a big relief and a lifesaver. Now I wouldn't have to write anything new.

Miya-san, though retired, is working even harder than before. Takahata is actively giving lectures around the country. As for myself, I plan to keep working as long as my services are seen to be of use, as long as Ghibli itself is needed.

Toshio Suzuki
May 2014

# Toshio Suzuki Chronology

**1948** August 19. Born in Nagoya, Aichi prefecture.

**1964** April. Matriculates at Tokai High School.

**1967** April. Matriculates at Keio University (literature faculty; sociology, psychology, and education major).

**1972** March. Graduates from Keio University (literature faculty).
March. Is hired by Tokuma Shoten Publishing, and assigned to the editorial department of *Shukan [Weekly] Asahi Geino*.

**1973** March. Is transferred to the editorial staff of *Komikku & Komikku* (Comic & Comic), a supplement to *Asahi Geino*, and becomes involved in the editing of a magazine featuring *gekiga*.

**1974** September. Begins working for the special features section of *Asahi Geino*, and is in charge of writing a weekly special feature.

**1975** October. Is transferred to the editorial department of the children's television magazine *Gekkan terebi rando* (Monthly TV Land).

**1978** May 26. The first issue of the monthly magazine *Animeju* (Animage), the July issue, is published. Suzuki is put in charge of editing from the initial issue. The first editor-in-chief was Hideo Ogata.

**1979** December 15. Under the direction of Hayao Miyazaki, *Rupan sansei: Kariosutoro no shiro* (The Castle of Cagliostro) is released, produced by Tokyo Movie Shinsha.

**1980** March. Suzuki is appointed copy editor at *Animage*.

**1981** April 11. *Jarinko Chie* (Chie the Brat), directed by Isao Takahata and produced by Tokyo Movie Shinsha, is released.
July. The feature article of the August issue of *Animage* is on Hayao Miyazaki.

**1982** January. Hayao Miyazaki's manga *Kaze no tani no Naushika* (Nausicaä of the Valley of the Wind) begins to be serialized in the February issue of *Animage*.
August. Suzuki is appointed vice editor-in-chief of *Animage*.

**1984** March 11. The animated film ***Kaze no tani no Naushika*** (Nausicaä of the Valley of the Wind ), directed by Hayao Miyazaki and produced by Topcraft, is released. Suzuki is listed in the credits as one of the production committee. From this time onward he begins to play a more substantial in film production.

**1985** June 15. The opening of Studio Ghibli in Kichijoji, Tokyo, takes place.

**1986** August 6. The Miyzaki-directed ***Tenku no shiro rapyuta*** (Castle in the Sky) is released, the first film to be produced by Studio Ghibli. Suzuki is listed as a member of the production committee.
October. Suzuki is appointed editor in chief of *Animage*.

**1988** April 16. A double feature consisting of ***Hotaru no haka*** (Grave of the Fireflies; directed by Isao Takahata) and ***Tonari no totoro*** (My Neighbor Totoro; directed by Hayao Miyazaki) is released, both produced by Studio Ghibli. Suzuki is listed in the credits as one of the production committee for the latter.

**1989** July 29. ***Majo no takkyubin*** (Kiki's Delivery Service), directed by Hayao Miyazaki and produced by Studio Ghibli, is released. Suzuki is listed in the credits as assistant producer; he was playing a greater role as a producer than heretofore.
October. Suzuki is sent on loan from Tokuma Shoten to work at Studio Ghibli. Studio Ghibli becomes the exclusive focus of his working hours.

**1990** November. Suzuki quits Tokuma Shoten and joins Studio Ghibli in December as company director.

**1991** July 20. ***Omoide poroporo*** (Only Yesterday), directed by Isao Takahata and produced by Studio Ghibli, is released. For the first time Suzuki is listed in the credits as the producer. From this point until (and including) *Kaze tachinu* (The Wind Rises), Suzuki acts as the producer in all of Ghibli's theatrical feature films.

**1992** May. Suzuki wins the 11th Fujimoto Prize, Special Award.
July 18. ***Kurenai no buta*** (Porco Rosso), directed by Hayao Miyazaki and produced by Studio Ghibli, is released.
August. The Ghibli studio in Koganei is completed, and the transfer made from Kichijoji.

**1994** July 16. ***Heisei tanuki gassen Ponpoko*** (Pom Poko), directed by Isao Takahata and produced by Studio Ghibli, is released.

**1995** July 15. ***Mimi o sumaseba*** (Whisper of the Heart), directed by Yoshifumi Kondo and produced by Studio Ghibli, is released. Hayao Miyazaki–directed short film ***On Your Mark*** runs before *Whisper of the Heart*.

**1995** December. Suzuki is appointed executive managing director of Studio Ghibli.

**1997** June. With the acquisition and merger of Ghibli by its parent company, Tokuma Shoten, Suzuki is appointed executive director of Tokuma Shoten and president of Studio Ghibli Company.
July 12. ***Mononoke-hime*** (Princess Mononoke), directed by Hayao Miyazaki and produced by Studio Ghibli, is released; the film breaks all box office records for a Japanese movie.
November. Suzuki wins the 14th Fumiko Yamaji Cultural Award.

**1998** March. As part of a Japanese TV program, Suzuki and Miyazaki set out to follow in the footsteps of Antoine de Saint-Exupéry in flying over the Sahara desert via France.
June. Suzuki wins the 17th Fujimoto Prize.

**1999** July 17. ***Hohokekyo tonari no Yamada-kun*** (My Neighbors the Yamadas), directed by Isao Takahata and produced by Studio Ghibli, is released.
September. Suzuki leaves for the United States to promote *Princess Mononoke* in North America.
October. With Tokuma Shoten's conversion from a company system to a divisional system, Suzuki is appointed executive director of operations of Studio Ghibli division at Tokuma Shoten.

**2000** March. The groundbreaking ceremony for the Ghibli Museum, Mitaka, is conducted at Inokashira Park.
September. The president of Tokuma Shoten, Yasuyoshi Tokuma, passes away. Suzuki is appointed executive managing director of Studio Ghibli division at Tokuma Shoten.
December. Hideaki Anno's live-action movie ***Shiki-Jitsu*** (ritual) is shown at the Tokyo Photography Museum, produced by Studio Kajino and Suzuki as executive producer.

**2001** July 20. ***Sen to Chihiro no kamikakushi*** (Spirited Away), directed by Hayao Miyazaki and produced by Studio Ghibli, is released. In November it surpasses *Titanic* (released in 1997) in box office revenue and establishes an all-time box office high for a film in Japan.
September. The Tokuma Memorial Cultural Foundation for Animation is established. Suzuki serves on the board of directors.
October 1. Ghibli Museum, Mitaka, opens to the public.
December. Suzuki travels to France to promote the release of *Spirited Away*.

**2002** February. Suzuki attends the 52nd Berlin International Film Festival, at which *Spirited Away* wins the Golden Bear (Grand Prix).
February. Suzuki wins the award for best producer at the Elan d'or Awards.

| | |
|---|---|
| **2002** | May. Suzuki wins the 21st Fujimoto Prize.<br>July 20. ***Neko no ongaeshi*** (The Cat Returns), directed by Hiroyuki Morita, and ***Giburizu episodo 2*** (the GHIBLIES episode 2), directed by Yoshiyuki Momose, are produced by Studio Ghibli as a double feature. Suzuki is in charge of character design for GHIBLIES episode 2.<br>September. Suzuki travels to the United States to promote *Spirited Away*.<br>November. Wins the First Japan Innovator Grand Prize. |
| **2003** | March. *Spirited Away* wins an Academy Award for Best Animated Feature at the 75th Academy Awards. |
| **2004** | March 6. ***Inosensu*** (Ghost in the Shell 2: Innocence), directed by Mamoru Oshii and produced by Production I.G., is released. Suzuki serves as co-producer.<br>April. Suzuki begins lecturing at the University of Tokyo as adjunct professor in the Content Creation and Management Course, Interfaculty Initiative in Information Studies, a position he will hold for five years.<br>September. Suzuki attends the 61st Venice International Film Festival. *Hauru no ugoku shiro* (Howl's Moving Castle) wins an Osella award.<br>November 20. ***Howl's Moving Castle,*** directed by Hayao Miyazaki and produced by Studio Ghibli, is released. From November into December Suzuki visits France and Great Britain to promote *Howl's Moving Castle.* |
| **2005** | March 31. Studio Ghibli, a division of Tokuma Shoten, becomes independent of the parent company and becomes the Studio Ghibli, Inc. Suzuki is appointed president.<br>April. Suzuki publishes his first book, *Eiga doraku* (Mixing Film with Pleasure), with Pia.<br>June. Suzuki visits the United States to promote *Howl's Moving Castle*. |
| **2006** | July 29. ***Gedo senki*** (Tales from Earthsea), directed by Goro Miyazaki and produced by Studio Ghibli, is released. |
| **2007** | January. Hideo Ogata, former executive managing director of Tokuma Shoten, passes away.<br>March. Suzuki wins the 2nd Shin Watanabe Prize.<br>October. Suzuki begins the radio program *Jiburi asemamire* (Sweating It Out at Ghibli), where he serves as host. |
| **2008** | February. Suzuki is appointed producer and chairman at Studio Ghibli.<br>July. Suzuki's book *Shigoto doraku: Sutajio Jiburi no genba* (Mixing Work with Pleasure: My Life at Studio Ghibli) is published by Iwanami Shinsho.<br>July 19. ***Gake no ue no Ponyo*** (Ponyo on the Cliff by the Sea), directed by Hayao Miyazaki and produced by Studio Ghibli, is released. |

**2010** March. The TV commercial for Nisshin Seifun Group featuring the cat Konyara, designed by Suzuki, begins to air.
July 17. ***Karigurashi no Arietti*** (Arrietty), directed by Hiromasa Yonebayashi and produced by Studio Ghibli, is released.
October. Suzuki wins the Tsumugi Prize at Asiagraph 2010.

**2011** March. Seiichiro Ujiie, chairman of Nippon Television Network Corporation, passes away.
July 16. ***Kokuriko-zaka kara*** (From Up on Poppy Hill), directed by Goro Miyazaki and produced by Studio Ghibli, is released.
August. Suzuki publishes *Jiburi no tetsugaku: Kawaru mono to kawaranai mono* (Ghibli's Philosophy: Things that Change and Things that Don't) with Iwanami Shoten.

**2012** June. Suzuki receives an honorary degree from the Rhode Island School of Design (RISD), together with Isao Takahata and Hayao Miyazaki.
July. ***Kyoshinhei Tokyo ni arawaru*** (A Giant Warrior Descends on Tokyo), directed by Shinji Higuchi and produced by Studio Ghibli in cooperation with Hideaki Anno, is shown at the Museum of Contemporary Art Tokyo exhibition "Director, Hideaki Anno's 'TOKUSATSU' Special Effects Museum—Craftsmanship of Showa & Heisei eras seen through miniatures." In November it is shown in a theatrical version together with *Shinseiki Evangerion* (Neon Genesis Evangelion: Q).
November. *Eiga doraku* is published in a small paperback size by Kadokawa Bunko.

**2013** March. *Suzuki Toshio no Jiburi asemamire 1* (Toshio Suzuki's Sweating It Out at Ghibli 1), based on the radio program, is published by fukkan.com. A sequal, *Suzuki Toshio no Jiburi asemamire 2,* is published in July.
July 20. ***Kaze tachinu*** (The Wind Rises), directed by Hayao Miyazaki and produced by Studio Ghibli, is released.
August. Suzuki's *Kaze ni fukarete* (Blown by the Wind) is published by Chuokoron-Shinsha.
November. *Suzuki Toshio no Jiburi asemamire 3* is published by fukkan.com.
November 23. ***Kaguya-hime no monogatari*** (The Tale of The Princess Kaguya), directed by Isao Takahata and produced by Studio Ghibli, is released. Suzuki is in charge of planning.
November. Suzuki wins the 58th Eiga no Hi special prize for meritorious service.
December. Suzuki visits the United States and Canada with Isao Takahata and others. Frédéric Back, John Lasseter, and others are given a preview screening of *The Tale of The Princess Kaguya.*

**2014** February–March. Travels to the United States to attend the 86th Academy Awards ceremony upon nomination of *The Wind Rises* as Best Animated Feature.
March. Suzuki awarded the 64th Annual MEXT Art Encouragement Prize.
May. Wins the 2nd Japan Advertising Federation Prize, Shoriki Award.
July. Release date of ***Omoide no Mani*** (When Marnie Was There), directed by Hiromasa Yonebayashi and produced by Studio Ghibli. Suzuki contributes to production as general manager.

(honorifics omitted)

# Bibliography

**Excerpted Works by Toshio Suzuki**

"Ima omoitsuku fuan-zairyo no are kore. Kore o kaisho shi, tadashii senden hoshin o kettei suru tame no memo aruiwa, Botamochi-san Manpuku-ji hondo hame-ita no itazura" (A Memo on Worrisome Things that I Have Noticed and How to Fix Them and Determine Correct Advertising Policy, or the Graffiti on the Wooden Panels at the Main Hall of Botamochi-san Manpuku-ji.) Internal memo. March 8, 1994.

"'Mimi o sumaseba' no senden o kangaeru ni atatte–aruiwa, kono nijunen no josei no chii ni tsuite" (Thinking about the Advertising for "Whisper of the Heart," or the Status of Women in the Last Twenty Years), internal memo, April 10, 1995.

*Sutajio Jiburi no junen* (Ten Years at Studio Ghibli), speech manuscript for Annecy International Animated Film Festival 1995.

"Eiga 'Mononoke-hime' setsumei shiryo" (Explanatory Material for the Film "Princess Mononoke"). Internal material. February 26, 1996.

"'Mononoke-hime' to iu taitoru" (The Title "Princess Mononoke"), *Dentsuho*, October 6, 1997.

"Tokuma shacho to Noma Hiroshi" (President Tokuma and Hiroshi Noma), pamphlet, 8th Japan Independent Film Festival, 2001.

"'Sen to Chihiro' wa Dizuni ni katta" ("Spirited Away" Beats Disney). Bungei Shunju, October, 2002.

"Miyazaki Hayao no johogen" (The Resources of Hayao Miyazaki), *Daigojukai minkan hoso zenkoku taikai kinen koen* (Memorial Lecture at the 50th Annual Convention of the Japan Commercial Broadcasters Association), November 25–26, 2002.

*Shinshun anime taidan: Suzuki Toshio vs. Oshii Mamoru* (New Year's Anime Dialogue: Toshio Suzuki vs. Mamoru Oshii), *Yomiuri* newspaper, January 1, 2004.

"'Senden o shinai 'senden'" ("Advertising" that Doesn't Advertise), press material for *Howl's Moving Castle*, 2004.

"Manga eiga to animeshon eiga" (Manga Films and Animated Films), in the catalog for *Nihon manga-eiga no zenbo-ten* (Japanese Animated Films: A Complete View from their Birth to "Spirited Away" and Beyond), held from July 15, 2004 at the Museum of Contemporary Art Tokyo.

"Koshi kondo no hito" (A Man Who Mixes Work with Pleasure), in *Ano hata o ute!*

*Animeju keppu-roku* (Fire on that Flag! The Bloody Chronicles of *Animage*), by Hideo Ogata, 2004.

"Eiga o ai-suru futari kara no eiga seisaku no susume" (Advice on Filmmaking by Two Movie Lovers), *Suzuki Toshio–Yamada Yoji taidan* (Conversations with Toshio Suzuki and Yoji Yamada), *Kinema Junpo*, late December issue, 2004.

*Eiga doraku* (Mixing Film with Pleasure), Pia, 2005.

"Eigazukuri mo ryutsu mo, jidai no kawarime ni bokura wa iru" (In Filmmaking and Distribution, We Reside at a Turn of the Times), *Neppu* (Hot Wind), dialogue between Toshio Suzuki and Yasuhiro Suzuki, Studio Ghibli, May 10, 2005 issue.

"Akai tsuchi" (Red Earth), press release for "Kazuo Oga Exhibition" opening on July 21, 2007 at the Museum of Contemporary Art Tokyo.

*Kaze ni fukarete* (Blown by the Wind), Chuokoron-Shinsha, 2013.

"'Ima' o tanoshimu" (Enjoying the "Moment"), in *Minna no negai* (Everyone's Wish), Japanese Association for the Study of Issues Faced by People with Disabilities, October 2013.

**Excerpted Works by Others**

Isao Takahata, interview, "Boku wa 'suketto' purodyusa nan desu" (I Serve as a Producer in a "Pinch,") in *Roman arubamu ekusutora kaze no tani no Naushika* (Roman Album Extra: Nausicaä of the Valley of the Wind), Tokuma Shoten, 1984.

Isao Takahata, "Gendai-jin zentai e no yuai monogatari" (A Tale of Fellow Feeling for All Modern Man), press announcement for *Castle in the Sky*, October 7, 1985, in *Jiburi roman arubamu Tenku no shiro Rapyuta* (Ghibli's Roman Album *Castle in the Sky*), Tokuma Shoten, 2001.

Isao Takahata, "Erosu no hibana" (The Fireworks of Eros), in *Shuppatsu-ten* (Starting Point), Hayao Miyazaki, Tokuma Shoten, 1996.

Isao Takahata, *Manga eiga no kokorozashi* (The Aspirations of Manga Films), Iwanami Shoten, 2007.

Isao Takahata, Hayao Miyazaki, and Toshio Suzuki. "Sutajio Jiburi sanjunen-me no hatsu teidan" (The First Trialogue in Ghibli's Thirtieth Year), in *Bungei Shunju*, February 2014.

Seiichiro Ujiie (interviewer, Yonematsu Shiono). *Showa to iu jidai o ikite* (My Life in the Showa Period), Iwanami Shoten, 2012.

Yoshiaki Nishimura and Nobuo Kawakami. "Densetsu no otoko, Takahata Isao, wa ikani kikan shita no ka?" (The Remarkable Return of the Legendary Isao Takahata), a dialogue in *Switch*, December 2013.

# About the Author

## Toshio Suzuki

Born in Nagoya city in 1948, Suzuki graduated from Keio University (literature faculty) in 1972 and was employed by Tokuma Shoten Publishing. After working in the editorial department of the magazine *Animage*, he became involved in film production with *Nausicaä of the Valley of the Wind*. From 1989 he devoted his time exclusively to Studio Ghibli, producing numerous hits such as *Princess Mononoke* and *Spirited Away*.

He is presently producer and chairman of Studio Ghibli.

His other publications include *Eiga doraku* (Mixing Film with Pleasure; Kadokawa Bunko), *Jiburi no tetsugaku* (Ghibli's Philosophy; Iwanami Shoten), *Suzuki Toshio no Jiburi asemamire* (Toshio Suzuki's Sweating It Out at Ghibli; fukkan.com), *Kaze ni fukarete* (Blown by the Wind; Chuokoron-Shinsha), and *Jinsei wa tannaru karasawagi: Kotoba no maho* (Life Is Nothing but a Fuss over Nothing: The Magic of Words; Kadokawa Shoten).

〈英文版〉仕事道楽 新版 スタジオジブリの現場
*Mixing Work with Pleasure: My Life at Studio Ghibli*

2018年3月27日　第1刷発行

著　者　鈴木 敏夫
訳　者　ロジャー・スピアズ
発行所　一般財団法人出版文化産業振興財団
〒101-0051 東京都千代田区神田神保町3-12-3
電話　03-5211-7282（代）
ホームページ　http://www.jpic.or.jp/

印刷・製本所　大日本印刷株式会社

定価はカバーに表示してあります。

Printed in Japan.
ISBN 978-4-86658-022-7